# Father
## & Child Companion

MQ Publications Limited
12 The Ivories, 6–8 Northampton Street
London N1 2HY
Tel: +44 (0) 20 7359 2244
Fax: +44 (0) 20 7359 1616
email: mail@mqpublications.com
www.mqpublications.com

Designer: Lindsey Johns

ISBN: 1-84072-808-6

10 9 8 7 6 5 4 3 2 1

Printed and bound in China

# Father
## & Child Companion

WYNN WHELDON

MQP

# Contents

# Introduction

This book is largely a celebration of fatherhood, but it is not just about dads: it is also about sons and daughters, mothers and families. Fatherhood is a role, not a personality. To be performed well, it requires the occasional subsuming of personality into something greater than oneself—the family. It can also involve a willingness to do things you don't want to do. It is both effortless and hard, both a delight and a struggle.

There are, of course, as many different kinds of father as there are fathers. There are those who love from a distance, and others who have a keen bond with their children; there are fathers who joke and fathers who demand an earnest response to the serious business of life; there are doting fathers and negligent fathers.

My own father never taught me how to shave, mend a fuse, build a kite, or light a barbecue. He was hopeless with tents. But he was a wonderful storyteller, and his stories were of the real, experienced world; and he had a laugh the size of an ocean. I certainly fought with him but I never for a moment believed he did not love me wholly and unconditionally. He was always on my side. The most important thing he taught me was never to despise the one life I have. Of course, I never told him how safe or big he made the world for me: we never do. I like to think he knew how I felt about him, but he was a modest man, who usually put the triumphs of family life down to my mother.

This book will be, I hope, a way of letting our fathers know how we feel about them. In an age when the role is perhaps more complicated than ever before, it becomes especially important not only for children to know they are loved, but for fathers to know it too. This book is designed to promote happiness.

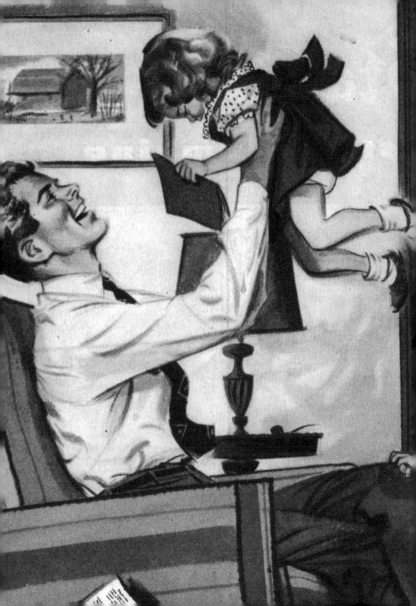

# A Father's Love

Can you remember the clinch of your father? The roughness of his pullover, the hint of stubble on his chin, the broken nose you traced a thousand times with your little finger, the curious outgrowings of his eyebrows, the faint suggestion of illicit tobacco mixed with soap. Do you recall the way he allowed you to mold the features of his face into comical grotesqueries, to squeeze his cheeks so that his mouth became a vertical opening? Do you remember him on all fours, crawling across your bedroom floor? Do you recall the grunts and roars and gnashings that gave you such delicious tremors of fear? Can you forget that he was the worst dragon of your imaginings, that you never moved faster in your life than when he pursued you upstairs? Can you still remember being hung upside down, the throwings, and the arm wrestles? Do you remember the clinch of your father, in which he said, not with words, but with a gesture, "I love you beyond all things, for you are what I have given the world, you are the best of me, you are for what I was made."

# Happy Househusbands

*"When I was a kid, I used to imagine animals running under my bed. I told my dad, and he solved the problem quickly. He cut the legs off the bed."*

LOU BROCK

The toughest part of househusbanding is probably the school run in the morning. Unless you are careful, then traditional male contempt for female driving abilities (or, rather, habits) can become ossified into rock-hard prejudice. Mothers like to get their children as close to school as they possibly can. If this means knocking over small pieces of street furniture (or dogs), cracking carefully laid sidewalks, or blocking traffic for a mile in all directions, then they will do it. Fathers loathe jams caused by mothers unconcerned by anything other than their own child's convenience. Yet the school-run jam is unavoidable: the househusband regularly has to sit it out, simmering gently, until he is in a position where he can release the child and watch him disappear through the school gate. By the time he gets home, he is in no mood for ironing.

For the househusband, ironing is a double hell, because in his opinion, at least half of the laundry didn't need doing in the first place. His children are not going to go down with cholera as a result of wearing the same shirt two days running. But his household has standards, and these are invariably set by his wife. Society does not seem to have developed to that point where a househusband wields the power that the housewife hitherto enjoyed. Ironing, with its geometrical impossibilities (how do you deal with a three-dimensional object by treating it as flat?) and frustrations (what exactly is the point of ironing underwear?) remains a task to be endured, not enjoyed (as bachelors are said to).

In most other respects, househusbanding is fairly straightforward as long as the father is prepared to accept responsibility for having put (hidden?) cuddly toy animals in the wrong places—"Just look under the bed, for heaven's sake." Cleaning chores can be niftily elided by a strong emphasis on tidiness. As for clothes washing, the househusband, if a techy, will enjoy hours in front of the increasingly complicated dials on the front of the washing machine. (For less fetishistic types, the rule is to do a "mixed wash" at 104°F—for everything.)

The afternoon school pick-up is the delicate time when the househusband must choose whether to join the mothers ☞

congregating at the school gate in order to gossip and scowl. Women appear to love outrage in the same way that men love laughter. They are liable to express shock at the hardly scandalous just as men guffaw at the hardly funny. (How outraged will female readers be at the above generalization? To a degree disproportionate to the perceived offence!) The househusband's role in these conversations is to take the ladies very seriously, without actually contributing any personal experience of his own (it will almost certainly contain humor, which is undesirable).

Even more than a single man needs it, even more than a married man needs it, the househusband needs an evening with his friends, drinking and laughing uproariously at the hardly funny. This can take place once a week, or once a month, but it must be done. It is the equivalent of the coffee mornings enjoyed by housewives. No breadwinning wife should deny its utter necessity; it will help keep her sane.

# "My father had a profound influence on me, he was a lunatic."

SPIKE MILLIGAN

# The Miracle of Birth

*"When Charles first saw our child Mary, he said all the proper things for a new father. He looked upon the poor little thing and blurted, 'She's more beautiful than the Brooklyn Bridge.'"*

HELEN HAYES

Many fathers nowadays feel it incumbent upon them to speak about the miracle of birth. From all quarters, fathers (especially movie stars) tell us that the birth of their children has been "the most beautiful thing they have ever seen." While not wishing to cast aspersions on the quality of their life events, this is an astonishing description of the agonising experience through which women go in order to deliver their partners such transcendental pleasure.

Childbirth is messy and painful. The father's impotence to help or alleviate the mother's suffering shows him, perhaps for the first time, that there are occasions when he is useless. Birth is of course miraculous, but who can blame the father who would prefer to pace the parking lot, wishing he had not given up smoking, instead of offering futile encouragement at the woman's side while she curses him for being a monster from the bowels of hell? But for the man who can stick it out, it's all worth it, of course—when he gets to see that squalling, red-faced bundle's first moments in the world, and redefine his own place in the world as a father, and experience love of a quite unexpected ferocity, a new man is born too.

Bye baby bunting

Daddy's gone a-hunting,

Gone to get a rabbit skin

To wrap the baby bunting in.

"Parents are the last people on Earth who ought to have children."

SAMUEL BUTLER

# Good Sleeping Practice

Many young children cry when they wake during the night. The following advice is by no means foolproof or mandatory, but it has been known to be an effective if daunting practice. A mother's response will often tend toward the soft-hearted and comforting, which only encourages the child to cry on waking. In this area of childcare, the masculine response can be particularly effective.

It is helpful for the father to show the child that crying will not immediately bring her mother, but instead, after a certain period, her father. The child should be left to cry for, say, ten minutes, before being attended to. As soon as the child is quiet (not necessarily asleep), she should be put back down, and left. If she cries again, wait another ten minutes.

In the second week, the period should be increased to twelve or fifteen minutes, and so on. Within a month, the child should have discovered that crying brings no rewards. (Older children who wake from nightmares should of course be comforted at once.)

During the weeks in which you are trying to instill in your child a sleep routine, it is likely that you won't get much sleep yourself—this is the price you will pay for eventual night-long peace. If you find yourself falling asleep at work, with a less than sympathetic boss, you might find the following excuse helpful: "Yes, they told me at the blood donor bank that this might happen."

EXTRACT FROM

# Anna Karenina

*by*

LEO TOLSTOY

Levin sat listening to the doctor's stories of a quack mesmerizer and looking at the ashes of his cigarette. There had been a period of repose, and he had sunk into oblivion. He had completely forgotten what was going on now. He heard the doctor's chat and understood it. Suddenly there came an unearthly shriek. The shriek was so awful that Levin did not even jump up, but, holding his breath, gazed in terrified inquiry at the doctor. The doctor put his head on one side, listened, and smiled approvingly. Everything was so extraordinary that nothing could strike Levin as strange. "I suppose it must be so," he thought, and still sat where he was. Whose scream was this?

Levin jumped up, ran on tiptoe to the bedroom, edged round Lizaveta Petrovna and the Princess, and took up his position at Kitty's pillow. The scream had subsided, but there was some change now. What it was he did not see and did not comprehend, and he had no wish to see or comprehend. But he saw it by the face of Lizaveta Petrovna. Lizaveta Petrovna's face was stern and pale, and still as resolute, though her jaws were twitching, and her eyes were fixed intently on Kitty. Kitty's swollen and agonized face, a tress of hair clinging to her moist brow, was turned to him and sought his eyes. Her lifted hands asked for his hands. Clutching his chill hands in her moist ones, she began squeezing them to her face.

"Don't go, don't go! I'm not afraid, I'm not afraid!" she said rapidly. "Mamma, take my earrings. They bother me. You're not afraid? Soon, soon, Lizaveta Petrovna…"

She spoke quickly, very quickly, and tried to smile. But suddenly her face was drawn—she pushed him away.

"Oh, this is awful! I'm dying, I'm dying! Go away!" she shrieked, and again he heard that unearthly scream.

Levin clutched at his head and ran out of the room.

"It's nothing, it's nothing, it's all right," Dolly called after him.

But they might say what they liked, he knew now that all was over. He stood in the next room, his head leaning against the doorpost, and heard shrieks, howls, such as he had never heard before, and he knew that what had been Kitty was uttering these shrieks. He had long ago ceased to wish for the child. By now he loathed this child. He did not even pray for her life now—all he longed for was the cessation of this awful anguish.

"Doctor! What is it? What is it? My God!" he said, snatching at the doctor's hand as he came up.

"It's the end," said the doctor. And the doctor's face was so grave as he said it that Levin took the end as meaning her death. ☞

Beside himself, he ran into the bedroom. The first thing he saw was the face of Lizaveta Petrovna. It was even more frowning and stern. Kitty's face he did not know. In the place where it had been was something that was fearful in its strained distortion and in the sounds that came from it. He fell down with his head on the wooden framework of the bed, feeling that his heart was bursting. The awful scream never paused, it became still more awful, and as though it had reached the utmost limit of terror, suddenly it ceased. Levin could not believe his ears, but there could be no doubt; the scream had ceased and he heard a subdued stir and bustle, and hurried breathing, and her voice, gasping, alive, tender, and blissful, uttered softly: "It's over!"

He lifted his head. With her hands hanging exhausted on the quilt, looking extraordinarily lovely and serene, she looked at him in silence and tried to smile, and could not.

And suddenly, from the mysterious and awful faraway world in which he had been living for the last twenty-two hours, Levin felt himself all in an instant borne back to the old everyday world, though glorified now by such a radiance of happiness that he could not bear it. The strained chords snapped; sobs and tears of joy which he had never foreseen rose up with such violence that his whole body shook, and for long they prevented him from speaking.

Falling on his knees before the bed, he held his wife's hand before his lips and kissed it, and the hand, with a weak movement of the fingers, responded to his kiss. And meanwhile, there at the foot of the bed, in the deft hands of Lizaveta Petrovna, like a flickering light in a lamp, lay the life of a human creature, which had never existed before, and which would now with the same right, with the same importance to itself, live and create in its own image.

"Alive! alive! And a boy too! Set your mind at rest!" Levin heard Lizaveta Petrovna saying, as she slapped the baby's back with a shaking hand.

"Mamma, is it true?" said Kitty's voice.

The Princess's sobs were all the answer she could make.

And in the midst of the silence there came in unmistakable reply to the mother's question, a voice quite unlike the subdued voices speaking in the room. It was the bold, clamorous, self-assertive squall of the new human being, which had so incomprehensibly appeared.

If Levin had been told before that Kitty was dead, and that he had died with her, and that their children were angels, and that God was standing before him, he would have been surprised at nothing. But now, coming back to the world of reality, he had to make great mental efforts to take in that she was alive and well, and that the creature squalling so desperately was his son. Kitty was alive, her agony was over. And he was unutterably happy. That he understood; and he was completely happy in it. But the baby? Whence, why, who was he?…He could not get used to the idea. It seemed to him something extraneous, superfluous, to which he could not accustom himself.

# Keeping up with the Kids

There is a father of a certain age who does not know where Beijing is, although he might hazard a guess at China. And if he were to come across this new place in a conversation with a son or daughter, he would ask mildly, "Where?" and he would be told: "You know! Beijing. Capital of China."

At this point the cogs of the father's brain will take in the fact that Peking has been replaced by Beijing, and the child will recoil in astonishment as his father erupts into a vehement attack either on the modern world and its fatuities, or on the linguistic pretensions of his offspring, but more probably both.

Once, the pronunciation of Marseilles rhymed with Wales. Now it rhymes (more or less) with Bombay. (Except now of course Bombay is Mumbai.) Livorno was once better known as Leghorn, and Ceylon was an island, not merely a variety of tea. Once he has exhausted his indignation, this is the kind of wistful way that the father will carry on. But we should not laugh too scornfully, for one day, Paris will rhyme with Marie, and Rome with Homer.

# Dad's Favorite Recipe: 1

## SPAGHETTI AND MEATBALLS

Spaghetti and meatballs is a firm favorite of both dads and kids alike. Easy to make, tasty, and filling, it's a great dish to serve the whole family!

**MEATBALLS**

2 tbsp olive oil
I onion, finely chopped
2 garlic cloves, crushed
2 tsp dried basil
I tsp dried oregano
$\frac{1}{2}$ tsp dried thyme
I cup/55g fresh white bread crumbs
$\frac{1}{4}$ cup/60ml whipping cream
I egg, lightly beaten
Ilb/450g ground (minced) beef
4oz/115g ground (minced) pork
4oz/115 ground (minced) veal
$\frac{3}{4}$ cup/55g grated Parmesan cheese
2 tbsp chopped parsley
salt and freshly ground black pepper

**1** First make the tomato sauce: heat the oil in a heavy-based saucepan over medium heat. Add the onion and cook, stirring occasionally, until softened, about 8 minutes. Add the garlic and cook 1 minute.

**2** Stir in the Italian tomato sauce, tomato paste, sugar, bay leaf, oregano, and basil. Bring to a boil, stirring occasionally, and season to taste with salt and pepper. Reduce the heat and simmer until slightly reduced and thickened, about 1 hour. Stir in the parsley.

**TOMATO SAUCE**
2 tbsp olive oil
1 onion, finely chopped
2 garlic cloves, crushed
4 x 15oz/425g cans Italian
    tomato sauce
12oz/350g tomato paste
1 tbsp brown sugar
1 bay leaf
1 tsp dried oregano
1 tsp dried basil
2 tbsp chopped parsley

**TO SERVE**
1 tbsp vegetable oil
1lb/450g spaghetti

**3** Meanwhile, prepare the meatballs: heat the oil in a frying pan over medium heat. Add the onion and cook until softened, stirring occasionally. Add the garlic, basil, oregano, and thyme, and season to taste; cook 1 minute longer. Remove from the heat and allow to cool.

**4** Put the bread crumbs in a bowl with the cream, and allow to stand until the cream is absorbed. Beat in the egg. Mix the ground beef, pork, and veal in a large bowl using a fork or your fingertips. Add the onion mixture, the soaked bread, about a third of the Parmesan, and the parsley. Mix until well combined.

**5** Shape the meat mixture into 1½in/4cm-meatballs. About 30 minutes before the tomato sauce is completely cooked, drop the meatballs into the simmering sauce and continue to cook, stirring occasionally.

**6** Bring a large saucepan three-quarters full of water to a boil. Add 1 tbsp salt and the oil. Add the spaghetti, stirring to separate the strands, and bring back to a boil. Cook for 8–10 minutes, until tender but still firm to the bite, or *al dente*. Drain and transfer to warmed serving bowls. Top with a little sauce and some meatballs. Serve with the remaining grated Parmesan.

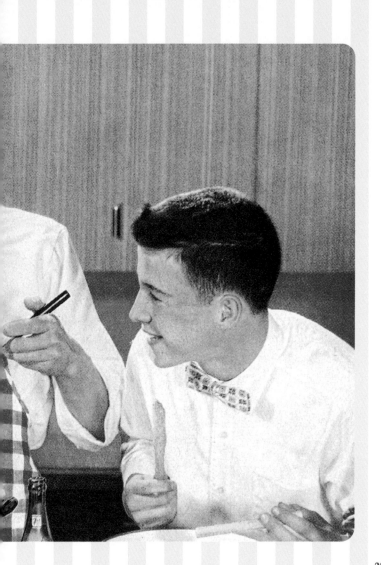

# Three Little Words

If you say the words "I love you" often enough, they will come easily. If a father says "I love you" to his sons and daughters every night, it will become habitual. (The danger of this is that if the habit is broken, the hurt will be extreme.) To the children, their father's "I love you" will seem as commonplace as "Goodnight." The children will grow up knowing that "I love you" isn't hard to say, and that you can say it every day. Maybe that's a good thing; maybe it isn't.

The great American novelist Henry James once said that a novelist should show, not tell. Translated into the language of fatherhood, this means that your children will know if you love them. No amount of "I love you" can make it true if it isn't. If you love your children, you will show them. You can't help that. They cannot help seeing. They don't need to be told. "I love you" will remain a hard and serious thing to say.

And the sanctity of those three little words, spoken with heartfelt rarity, will be no more apparent than when you hear your own children say them back to you for the first time.

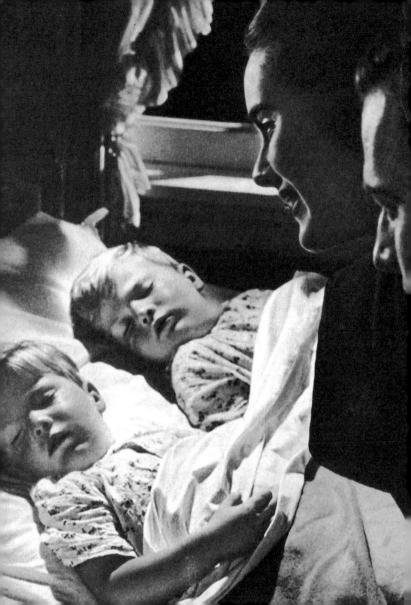

# Sleeping Beauties

How irresistible children are when they sleep. The least
burdensome weight on earth is the weight of your sleeping
child. Perhaps you are holding her, her head on your
shoulder, your arm beneath her rump. Or maybe you are
on a lawn in summer, and she will be lying on you, merely
restful. Here is a moment so perfect that it seems to exist
outside the imperfect life you lead. The illusion that you can
provide utter security is total. Here is complete trust. In your
arms, between your walls, your child is safe. Having put the
child down, and having covered her as delicately as
snowflakes cover a petal, you may sit and look on the calm
expressions of sleep, and wonder how someone as
imperfect as yourself has contributed to the making of a
creature as pure as this. This only has to happen once for life
to have been worth living.

Cherish this blissful serenity for as long as possible,
because you know that when they wake up, your children
become slightly less peaceful and slightly livelier…

# Kid's Party

To arrange a successful party for a bunch of five-year-olds, you need a Buddhist disregard for material possessions, the competence of Florence Nightingale, the military discipline of Julius Caesar, and the powers of entertainment of Harpo Marx. If you possess all these qualities, your child's birthday party will go swimmingly. If you don't, it will be a very long two hours.

As in all major projects or operations, success lies in the planning. Mothers are very good at this, and it is generally their orbit; it is up to you, as a father, to put the plan into effect, to police, officiate, and entertain.

The party is likely to start at about three o'clock. But be prepared for the doorbell to ring half an hour earlier, because that is when the first mother will show. It is possible that you will get your first extra guest at this time, because little Jimmy's cousin Beelzebub is staying with him... ☞

You will of course smile welcomingly, and say, "Fine—the more the merrier." (Hint: prepare extra going-home gifts in advance—these usually take the form of bags filled with disgusting candy and cheap toys.) This mother won't stay, of course, and she may be a bit late collecting her boys after the party (it all depends on whether her tennis match goes to three sets, but she won't say this). Other mothers will stay, however, and so it is wise to have some wine in the fridge.

Within half an hour, your house will be overrun by what seems like thousands of small, noisy creatures dashing about in every direction at once. You attempt to round them up and try to play games with them. Beelzebub leads a dissenting faction that doesn't want to play blindman's bluff. He prefers something along the lines of kicking girls in the shins. You try more games. Beelzebub complains that he hasn't won a prize. You have been saving the game of pass the parcel until after the birthday lunch, but you are running out of games, so out comes that boulder of newspaper, a toy beneath each layer. "It wasn't like that in my day," all the parents mutter. It's over in a flash.

As your plans begin to go awry you desperately move through your repertoire of entertainment, from magic tricks that don't work, to bubble-blowing and quite useless attempts to make everyone sing together. An eternity passes and then you realize it is only four o'clock and there is still the birthday lunch (also known in some quarters as "war") to come, and after that—what?

Avoid serving food that requires silverware. Spoons, especially, serve very well as catapults. This of course means not having jello, which might be sad, but is certainly very wise. Sandwiches (of the 90 percent uneaten by the children, approximately 50 percent will be eaten by the parents, and the rest will be distributed in various ways on the floor, walls, and furniture of your home), potato chips, and cake will suffice. Your child will, of course, dissolve into floods of tears after Beelzebub blows out the candles on the cake before it has even reached the table.

After lunch (make it last as long as you possibly can) corral the party into a single space once more, for having left the table, they will have dispersed wantonly around the house. Beelzebub, for instance, will be attempting to insert his cake into the DVD player in the bedroom, or will be picking through the pile of gifts you have carefully hidden under the desk in your study, shaking each one for clues to its contents. (Hint: don't allow the presents to be opened until everyone has left, and keep a note of who has given what.)

By now you will be trying to wipe noses and faces and comfort Beelzebub's latest victim at the same time as you vainly attempt to distract the children with fun stuff. The last forty-five minutes flies by like an epoch.

Actually, there is no reason why a children's birthday party shouldn't be thoroughly enjoyable. There are two important rules: don't let the children get bored and don't ask them questions. Final hint: don't show them a balloon until the end, when you can fill the whole place with balloons, beat a retreat, and allow the children to go wild.

# Fun Project: 1

## MAKE AN ASTRONAUT JETPACK

**MATERIALS**

Large cereal box

Gray + black paint + paintbrushes

2 plastic bottles with tops

Paper or thin card, about 6-in/15-cm square

Assorted lids (small jars, bottles)

Styrofoam or frozen pizza backing, about 4 x 10in/10 x 25cm

Matchbox

Black + silver marker pens

Silver, black, white, number stickers

Scrap of coiled, thin wire

Small bead

Fabric or webbing, 2 strips each about 2 x 20in/5 x 50cm

Aluminum foil

Packing tape or clear tape

Scissors

Glue

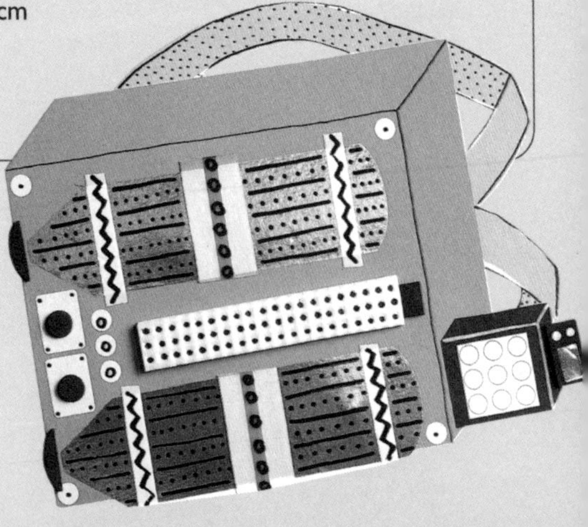

1 Tape the lid of the cereal box shut. Paint the box gray.

2 Cover the bottles with foil. Glue the bottles onto the box, with tops facing down. Cut 6 strips of paper about $\frac{3}{4}$ x 6in/2 x 15cm. Decorate using stickers or silver and black marker pens. Glue a strap over the top, middle and bottom of each bottle.

3 Thread the bead onto the wire. Tape the wire to the matchbox. Glue the matchbox to the top of the box. Paint the matchbox black. Glue a strip of styrofoam between the bottles. Add dials and control buttons with stickers, marker pen, and glued-on painted lids.

4 Tape or glue the fabric strips onto the box so you can wear it like a backpack.

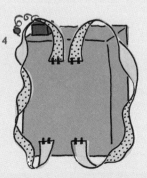

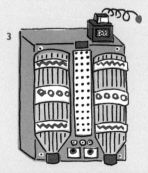

Whistle, daughter, whistle,
And you shall have a sheep.
Father, I cannot whistle,
Neither can I sleep.

Whistle, daughter, whistle,
And you shall have a cow.
Father, I cannot whistle,
Neither know I how.

Whistle, daughter, whistle,
And you shall have a man.
Father, I cannot whistle,
But I'll do the best I can.

AMERICAN FOLK SONG

# Fresh Air and Priorities

He wanted his son and daughter to grow up breathing clean air, in the company of children whose parents wanted the same. He wanted them to grow up in a community that cared for its children, and saw the future in them.

He was a workaholic—he felt most comfortable working, as though work was what he was meant to do. And to work he needed to live in the filthy air of the city, surrounded by the careless and the uncared for.

It was time to work out his priorities. He had to decide what he wanted most. He had to listen to what his wife wanted. She too wanted clean air for her children. They decided to move out of the city, and live for their children. When he looked at his family, he was amazed at how wholly enjoyable they were, and how they made his world bigger when he had thought they would make it smaller.

The decision was not difficult, yet it was fraught with anxiety. How would he keep the family finances fluid? How would he live without the company of friends he loved, and whom he knew loved him? He did not know, but he knew what his priorities were, and from that he drew strength. Within a year the health and happiness of his family showed him that the heart must sometimes be allowed to rule the head.

"To become a father is not difficult,
but to be a father is."

ANONYMOUS

# Le Père Goriot

*by*

HONORÉ DE BALZAC

"M. Goriot, how is it that your daughters have such fine houses, while you live in such a den as this?"

"Dear me, why should I want anything better?" he replied, with seeming carelessness. "I can't quite explain to you how it is; I am not used to stringing words together properly, but it all lies there—" he said, tapping his heart. "My real life is in my two girls, you see; and so long as they are happy, and smartly dressed, and have soft carpets under their feet, what does it matter what clothes I wear or where I lie down of a night? I shall never feel cold so long as they are warm; I shall never feel dull if they are laughing. I have no troubles but theirs. When you, too, are a father, and you hear your children's little voices, you will say to yourself, 'That has all come from me.' You will feel that those little ones are akin to every drop in your veins, that they are the very flower of your life (and what else are they?); you will cleave so closely to them that you seem to feel every movement that they make. Everywhere I hear their voices sounding in my ears. If they are sad, the look in their eyes freezes my blood. Some day you will find out that there is far more happiness in another's happiness than in your own. It is something that I cannot explain, something within that sends a glow of warmth all through you. In short, I live my life three times over. Shall I tell you something funny? Well, then, since I have been a father, I have come to understand God. He is everywhere in the world, because the whole world comes from Him. And it is just the same with my children, monsieur. Only, I love my daughters better than God loves the world, for the world is not so beautiful as God Himself is, but my children are more beautiful than I am. Their lives are so bound up with mine that I felt somehow that you would see them this evening. Great Heaven! If any man would make my little Delphine as happy as a wife is when she is loved, I would black his boots and run on his errands. That miserable M. de Marsay is a cur; I know all about him from her maid. A longing to wring his neck comes over me now and then. He does not love her! does not love a pearl of a woman, with a voice like a nightingale and shaped like a model. Where can her eyes have been when she married that great lump of an Alsatian? They ought both of them to have married young men, good-looking and good-tempered—but, after all, they had their own way."

Father Goriot was sublime. Eugène had never yet seen his face light up as it did now with the passionate fervor of a father's love....In the old man's tones and gesture there was something just then of the same spell that a great actor exerts over his audience. But does not the poet in us find expression in our affections?

# Bad Habits

Just because your adorable baby daughter has bitten you on the ear, it doesn't mean she's taken a dislike to you. It's just one little bad habit you're going to have to live with for a while.

What if she starts to pick her nose while watching cartoons on television? Well, this merely indicates that what she has up her nose is more interesting than cartoons. So either turn off the TV, because it is promoting too much nose-picking in your young innocent, or go and mend the garden fence. For peace and harmony, choose the second option.

Should the TV provoke your child to start hurling her head against it, be pleased by her discerning judgment, but do not allow your pleasure to show. On the whole, headbanging should be discouraged, though this is difficult in households where Ozzy Osbourne is revered.

Bad habits usually die out. Biting and headbanging will have more or less disappeared by the time a child is three. However, feeding tidbits to pets at the dinner table is one habit that a child will take with her well into maturity, and which you as a parent may well also succumb to, in mutual affection for the family pet. As for nose-picking, unfortunately this endures: it's the world's favorite occupation at red traffic lights.

# Starting School

It's your daughter's first day at elementary school. You've been building up to this gradually, preparing her gently. It's a big moment. On the day itself she wakes easily, eagerly, and jumps into her clothes.

As you walk the quarter mile to school she is happy; she chatters between the two of you, the proud and anxious parents. She has plans for making friends. And thankfully Charlie, her friend from kindergarten, will be there. You reach the melee at the school gates. You look at her mother. Her mother looks at you.

"See you," says your daughter merrily and disappears confidently into the throng. You put your arm around your wife's shoulders, and tell her you love her, because you are proud, and sad, and moved; you need her support, and she needs yours.

That evening you return from work. Your daughter dashes at you.

"How was school?" you ask.

"Wicked!"

You look at her mother, who shrugs in affectionate resignation. There are now to be others in her life—those who use the word "wicked" instead of "cool."

"Great!" you say, relieved, thinking that school is not going to be so traumatic after all.

The following morning you gently wake her again. She opens sleepy eyes. "Time to get up," you whisper.

"Why?" she asks. You smile knowingly. You remember this.

"You have to go to school."

"Silly Daddy," she says, and before turning back into her pillow, "I've been to school. I went yesterday."

# The Little League

It is the morning of the Little League baseball final, and your child is not yet awake. Should you wake him (a) so that he can enjoy the morning of the final, (b) because otherwise his biorhythms are going to be out of sync, (c) because he should have a large, sustaining breakfast, or (d) because it's about time the idle good-for-nothing was up anyway? Actually, the real reason you want to wake the child up is so that you can enjoy the morning of the final—so that you can advise, chivvy, encourage, and generally carry on until the kid says, "Dad, please stop talking."

A father is always very much more excited about a final than his child, because he probably wants to win it even more than the child does; he wants the reflected glory, but more than this he wants the child to be happy. A happy child makes life especially delightful and, in the end, this is all that men really want—happy people around them, especially close family members.

Once the final starts the father is caught in a horrible web of conflicting desires. Should he continue to advise, chivvy, and encourage (which he knows drives his child insane) and if so, how? Loudly, or merely on those occasions when the child is within reasonable earshot? Or should he be critical, a ruse to rile the child into passion? To what extent should he disparage or praise the opposition? Should he laugh or cry if the child's team is behind?

Then comes the greatest catastrophe of all: substitution. Only mothers can really deal with this, for their sympathies lie unconditionally with the fruit of their womb; with no compunction whatsoever they will attack, physically if need be, the team coach. For a mother, it is not a matter of judgment or the good of the team; the father, on the other hand, must put himself into the mind of the coach, and sometimes, horrifying as it might be, he will agree that another player should be substituted for his child. And then the father will be beset with terrible thoughts about his treachery against his own flesh and blood. Worse still, the child will be unhappy, and there is nothing whatsoever that can be done to alleviate his misery.

The father is then condemned to days, possibly weeks, of sleepless nights, wondering what the Right Thing To Do would have been. But all of you fathers can rest assured that there is very rarely only one Right Thing To Do. You were there and that's what counts.

# L GAME

**PARKER BROTHERS**

INCORPORATED

**SALEM, MASS.**

U.S.A.

# Anxiety and Pride

It was the first time the boy had traveled home from school on his own. For a long time he had begged to be allowed to do this, but circumstances had dictated against it. Now, at last, this wish was granted.

His father had been delighted at his son's insistence. It was to be encouraged, this independence. What's more, it would give the father more time for work. Every day, for years, he had picked up his son when school finished in mid-afternoon.

However, when the time came around to three o'clock that day, the father found he could not concentrate, visualizing his son in his mind's eye. Thirty minutes ticked by. Now the boy would be leaving school. Waiting for the bus.

The father could not help himself. He laid down his work and walked to the stop where his son would alight. A bus came. As it approached, he decided to remove himself from immediate view. He was suddenly aware that his son probably didn't want his father waiting for him, and might be embarrassed in front of his friends. He waited behind a chestnut tree.

The bus stopped. The boy got off. He began to walk home, past the chestnut tree. As he approached the tree, his father moved into his path. The father saw the boy's face crack into a delighted smile. The father was surprised by the joy he provoked, and tears filled his eyes. He had just enough time to compose himself as the boy ran toward him.

The father had felt anxious because he thought he was needed, but now he knew he was not needed, but loved.

# Surviving Sleepovers

One of the worst punishments a wife can impose on a disobliging husband is to allow the children to invite their friends for a sleepover. This is more or less synonymous with sleep deprivation. The word "sleepover" also brings to mind an image of those enormous underground tunnels where quarks, baryons, deltas, and protons are dashed together in a chaos of particle physics, every element traveling at roughly a zillion miles per hour. A sleepover allows you to conduct much the same kind of experiment in an average domestic setting at a tiny fraction of the cost.

Although you know it's insane, you have to provide filmed entertainment featuring mythic creatures of devastating destructive power (ancient or modern), and a midnight feast that includes cola and candy. If you don't, the kids will whine at you until bedtime, then refuse to sleep because they're not allowed their sugar shots. The fact is they're not going to go to sleep anyway, due to the combustible combination of excitement, caffeine, and the large quantities of candy that at least one of them will have smuggled in, so you may as well give in early, and plump for being a willing slave rather than an impotent master.

The sleepover is an opportunity for licensed naughtiness; for the guests it is like being at home without any of the rules of home; for the host it is an opportunity to show how easy it is to manipulate his parents or, very much more rarely, to demonstrate his parents' utter coolness (pretty much the same thing, actually).

The only way for you, as a parent, to survive a sleepover is to accept it as punishment, thereby reminding yourself in a terrifically adult way that there are consequences for your actions. You will probably only get to go to bed some time after 3:00 a.m., when that boy with the precocious disposition has finally stopped screaming inanities in your son's ear and giggling at a pitch sufficient to break expensive crystalware, and dropped off to sleep nowhere near his own sleeping bag, with chocolate smeared down one side of his face.

Needless to say, sleepovers can be chaotic and exhausting. Should you require a mantra to say on your occasional bathroom breaks or hastily snatched naps in the gazebo at the end of the backyard, the four wisest words in the universe are handy: "This too shall pass."

# Adventures with a Stroller

When a child gets to one or two years old, the baby carriage can be dumped in favor of a stroller. Weekdays are best for outings with the stroller, because there are fewer people around, and you can be alone with your child.

The outing may start off rigorously if you have to carry the stroller down several flights of stairs. It is probably not wise to do this with the child in the stroller at the same time, but, hey, you're a father, and strong—your child is safe with you. At the foot of the stairs you take a moment to recover. Explain this to your child. The child will stare up at you with a mixture of admiration and bemusement. That's fine: that's communication.

Set off with a clear destination in mind; don't make it too far, because it will take you much longer than you expect. Decide, say, to go to the local park via the bakery. Passing a construction site on your route can be quite educational for your child, who is bound to point in wonder at a revolving cement mixer, gurgling "mentmix" if especially advanced, or simply gurgling little, bubbly, spittle-words.

When at last you are able to escape the mesmerizing charms of the cement-mixer, stop at the bakery to buy yourself

a delicacy and your child an "indelicacy" such as a pretzel.
Pretzels are absolutely adored by teething children; they regard
them not as food but as edible toys. Mulched pretzel dough can
be guaranteed to dry to the consistency of cement on mini
designer dungarees. It also attaches itself, limpet-like, to the
child's face, especially around the corners of the mouth. This
doesn't really matter. Cleaning the child on returning home will
give you something to do for at least an hour.

The pretzel and delicacy can be consumed in the park. You
can sit by the big round pond that is covered with lilies and
croaking frogs, saying, "Look at the baby froggies," while your
child distributes the pretzel over face, hands, chair, and clothes,
with no interest whatsoever in nature's extraordinary variety.
What the child is dreaming of is the cement-mixer. So, hell, why
not go back that way? Before you know it, the morning has
passed; you have encouraged your offspring to breathe fresh air,
allowed him to commune with nature, and demonstrated the
unspeakable simplicity of the pretzel. The child is happy because
he has watched a cement mixer turning for forty-five minutes.
The world is a wonderful place. Now for lunch.

"Sweet to the father is his first-born's birth."

LORD BYRON

# Sweet Sixteen

Her room, even she can see (though she would never admit it) is a tip. Her father has had enough. She defies him over this as she has defied him over a whole catalog of teenage misdemeanors during the past week.

"It's a disgrace. How dare you be so slovenly? Who do you expect to clean this place up? I know who—you expect your mother to do it."

"It's my room, I can do what I want in it."

"No, actually it's my room. You can do what you like in your own house when you have one."

The row goes on. He leaves her weeping profusely.

Half an hour later, he returns. She is still crying. She has made some desultory attempts to remedy the horror of her bedroom. He is exasperated. He leaves her to it without a word.

An hour later she is still crying. He stands at the doorway of the room. It is festooned with the tawdry effects of popular culture: posters of celebrities, photos of happy times with innumerable friends, and piles of glossy magazines. He looks at his daughter and knows that she is not crying because of him.

"You're not crying because I was angry."

"No."

He sits down next to her, and waits for her to speak. Her boyfriend has left her. She tells him all about it: it is uncharacteristic of her, but there is such a tenderness in him, she trusts him. He listens. And then, all of a sudden, she is embarrassed, and becomes aware of what she is saying.

"It'll be alright," she mumbles.

"No," he says. "It won't be alright."

"No, it'll be fine Dad, really."

"My darling girl, it's never alright unless you make it alright. You must make it alright yourself."

"OK Dad."

He knows that she wants the conversation to be over.

Decades later, in similar circumstances, she will recall his words and understand them. She trusted her father because he told her what was true, and not merely what she wanted to hear, and now she misses him. She remembers his tender pragmatism when she was most vulnerable, and this comforts her, and she begins to remake herself.

# Dear Daddy

Soon after your father dies, it may be that one quiet afternoon, in a house emptier than ever before, you walk into his room, and you go through his things. You feel you are trespassing, but you are compelled. The things you find, the things that were his, feel somehow redundant, however potentially useful they might be. A screwdriver, a pen, a compass; you are looking for an item to remember him by. Here there is a selection of shoe horns, in bakelite, wood, and plastic. You will never use these. You don't know anyone who uses shoehorns. But you have a fancy for one. Or perhaps a pair of cufflinks. And of course the older you are, the greater your awareness of how useless this stuff actually is. You may wear a pair of cufflinks maybe six more times in your life, if you're lucky. Or maybe now is the time to take up wearing this elegant sartorial accessory? In the same drawer you find a stash of old foreign coins and metal lapel pins of obscure provenance. There are paperclips, golf tees, and empty cigar tubes. And somehow they combine to emit an aroma of the past, of what has been.

Then, tucked away among erratically hoarded tickets, folded so that the creases have become dark, you come upon a note you recognize as written in your own infant hand. It reads: "Dear Daddy, I love you and yore genral nollege and good serprizes."

And you want to cry, but instead you smile at this one last serprize.

"What a dreadful thing it must be to have a dull father."

MARY MAPES DODGE

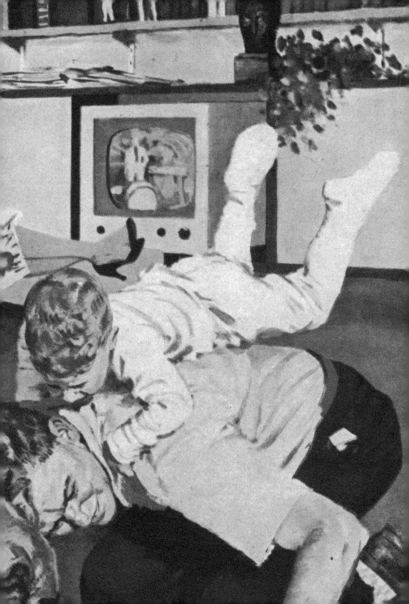

# Fun Project: 2

## MAKE A VOLCANO

Follow these simple instructions to make your very own volcano—
then stand back and watch it erupt right before your eyes! This project
is great fun whatever your age and also provides a wonderful
opportunity to teach older children some basic science and geography.
It can get very messy though, so make sure you wear old clothes and
spread out some newspaper beneath you before you start.

**MATERIALS**

1 small plastic bottle
1 square of cardboard
   (approx. 20-in/50-cm
   square)
Masking tape
1 cup/150g flour
Water
1 large bowl
Lots of old newspaper
Paint in various colors
1 cup vinegar
Red food coloring
4 tbsp baking soda

**1** Hold the plastic bottle in the center of the cardboard and use the masking tape to fix it in place. Run several strips of the tape from the top of the bottle to various points near the edge of the cardboard, trying to space the strips evenly apart and at equal distances from the bottle.

**2** Put the flour in a large bowl and mix in the water, a little at a time, until the paste is the consistency of thick glue. Add a little more flour, if necessary, to thicken.

**3** Tear the newspaper into strips approximately 1 in-wide. Dip the newspaper strips into the mixture one at a time, then lay them between the strips of masking tape. Repeat this process, slightly overlapping the strips and building up the layers until the whole structure, except for the bottle opening, is covered in papier mâché.

**4** Leave it to dry overnight, and then paint it to resemble a volcano.

**5** Wait for the paint to dry, and then pour the vinegar into the open top of the volcano with approximately 10 drops of the red food coloring.

**6** When you are ready to see your volcano explode, pour in all of the baking soda in one swift movement. Then step back and watch the fun!

# Five Famous Fathers

There is a very tender moment in Greek legend when Hector, son of King Priam of Troy, a supreme warrior, is about to face certain death at the hands of the vengeful and unbeatable Achilles. He bids his wife and son goodbye, removing his helmet in order not to frighten the baby.

The arch-guru of the Enlightenment, Swiss-born Jean-Jacques Rousseau, compares very poorly against Hector. Rousseau expressed the need for man to be released from the chains that bind him—a theme he also applied to his home life, by farming out his five children to foundling hospitals.

Charles Darwin, a man whose precise observation of the world puts Rousseau to shame, but who gets blamed for much that Rousseau was responsible for, was a profoundly loving father, and familiarly so. "He is so charming," he wrote of his five-month-old son, "that I cannot pretend to any modesty. I defy anybody to flatter us on our baby, for I defy anyone to say anything in its praise of which we are not fully conscious."

Charles Dickens' books abound with waifs, orphans and strays, fathers, and father figures. His daughter wrote that she held him "in her heart of hearts."

But you don't have to be a good father to produce a great son. Indeed, wartime British Prime Minister Winston Churchill thought the opposite. His own father Randolph was so distant that Winston described himself as being "deprived of a father's care," but at the same time ascribed his independence of mind, and his powerful will to succeed, to this very cause.

Right: Charles Dickens with his daughters

# The Iliad

*by*

HOMER

Hector smiled as he looked upon the boy, but he did not speak, and Andromache stood by him weeping…

He stretched his arms towards his child, but the boy cried and nestled in his nurse's bosom, scared at the sight of his father's armor, and at the horse-hair plume that nodded fiercely from his helmet. His father and mother laughed to see him, but Hector took the helmet from his head and laid it all gleaming upon the ground. Then he took his darling child, kissed him, and dandled him in his arms, praying over him the while to Jove and to all the gods. "Jove," he cried, "grant that this my child may be even as myself, chief among the Trojans; let him be not less excellent in strength, and let him rule Ilius with his might. Then may one say of him as he comes from battle, 'The son is far better than the father.' May he bring back the blood-stained spoils of him whom he has laid low, and let his mother's heart be glad."

With this he laid the child again in the arms of his wife, who took him to her own soft bosom, smiling through her tears.

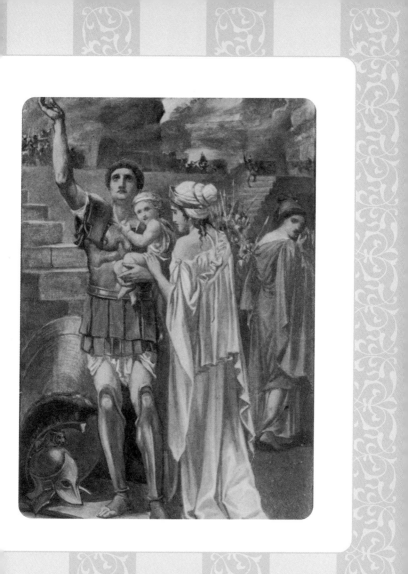

"It doesn't matter who my father was;
it matters who I remember he was."

ANNE SEXTON

# Papa, Always and Forever

The word "papa" must be one of the earliest words ever uttered. It has been handed down over tens of thousands of years, passing into a great number of vastly differing languages. Some linguists believe that the word "papa" proves the existence of a single original language. Others say it is merely one of the first sounds a baby is able to make.

"Papa," or a recognizable variant, existed in well over half the thousand languages studied in a recent survey. For example, in African Swahili, "mother" and "father" are "mama" and "baba"; this is precisely the same as in Chinese Mandarin; Bengali differs only in that it employs only one "ma." In Malay, "father" is "bapa," while in Apalai, spoken by Amazonian Indians, the words for "mother" and "father" are "aya" and "papa."

"Dad" or "Daddy"—although only recorded in English as late as 1500—is probably similarly ancient and nearly universal. In Welsh it is "Tad," in Irish "Daid," in Czech, Latin, and Greek it is "Tata," in Lithuanian "Tete," and in Sanskrit "Tatah." The expression "daddy-o" first appears in 1949, used by the beat generation.

Our modern English "father" is a direct descendent of the Greek word "pater," passing through the Old German "fater," and Old English "faeder."

It has been argued that the ancient Persian word "pa," meaning "foot" or "leg," is the origin of the Greek word "pater." Small children, it is suggested, called their father "Pa" because they could see his legs, whereas their mother's legs were hidden beneath a long skirt—a sweet, if doubtful etymology.

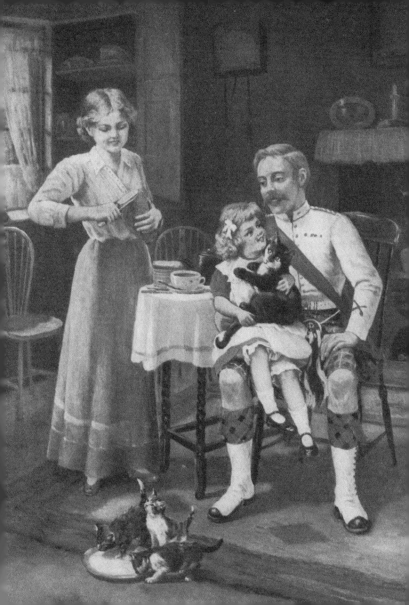

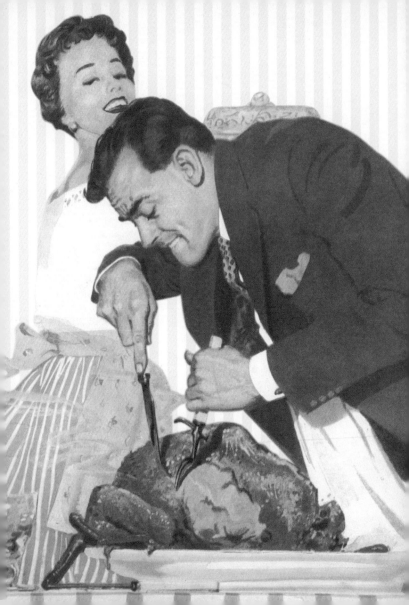

# Carving the Roast

It is the classic image of twentieth-century patriarchy: the father standing at the head of the table, brandishing a carving knife above the sacrificial beast, his children and spouse looking on with awe. It is the perfect opportunity for the father to demonstrate his role as head of the household, as the family's protector and provider.

Men are fascinated by the technicalities of carving roast meat. First the blade must be sharpened, with a flurry of graceful movement, like that of an orchestral conductor. Then the first satisfying cut can be made. There is a dedicated approach to carving a roast. For a turkey or chicken, the limbs are first removed, and then the breast sliced inward to the backbone; beef is cut thinly, pork is served in chunky slices, and lamb is distributed in large, fat slices.

Using the carving fork, the father doles out the pieces onto the plates before him. He looks happy: he has hunted, gathered, and now served. He has earned his food. He takes a slurp of decent quality claret, fills his wife's glass, and lets his children mix a thimbleful with water. No point in wasting the stuff.

# Mowing the Lawn

Many fathers, perhaps the majority, are gadget-loving men. When it comes to the task of mowing the lawn, they delight in using the latest technological marvel to complete the chore with the minimum of effort.

Other fathers prefer to mow the lawn by hand, which is to say with an old, slightly blunt-bladed, reel or cylinder mower. A hand mower does not chew the grass in the way sheep do; nor does it rip it the way a scythe does; and it does not shatter it the way a rotary mower does. It cuts it, as scissors do. The first patent for such an instrument—a "machine for mowing lawns, etc."—was granted to Edwin Beard Budding from Stroud, England, on August 31, 1830.

The puritan ethos betrays itself here perhaps more starkly than anywhere else. After all, your father is quite happy to use cars, trains, planes, dishwashers, hi-fi systems, and TV sets. Why not use something up-to-date in the garden? It is an unexplained but familiar phenomenon.

Indeed there is something thrilling about seeing your father's naked torso toiling with a traditional lawnmower, the sweat running down his body in discrete rivulets, as in a jungle after a tropical storm. Only on the beach will you also witness your father in this state of undress. You will come to enjoy mowing day because the work puts him in a very good mood, full of moral virtue. He has toiled honestly, and he is magnanimous toward one and all. This will teach you that labor is good for the soul.

# Father and Son

*from*

THE PERCY ANECDOTES

*by*

REUBEN AND SHOLTO PERCY

Among the cases of suffering by the wreck, in 1686, of the vessel in which the Siamese embassy to Portugal was embarked, few have stronger claims to pity than that of the captain. He was a man of rank, sprung from one of the first families in Portugal; he was rich and honorable, and had long commanded a ship in which he rendered great service to the king his master, and had given many marks of his valor and fidelity. The captain had carried his only son out to India along with him; he was a youth possessed of every amiable quality, well instructed for his years: gentle, docile, and most fondly attached to his father. The captain watched with the most intense anxiety over his safety: on the wreck of the ship, and during the march to the Cape, he caused him to be carried by his slaves. At length all the slaves having perished, or being so weak that they could not drag themselves along, this poor youth was obliged to trust to his own strength, but became so reduced and feeble that having laid him down to rest on a rock, he was unable to rise again. His limbs were stiff and swollen, and he lay stretched at length unable to bend a joint. The sight struck like a dagger to his father's heart; he tried repeatedly to recover him, and by assisting him to advance a few steps, supposed that the numbness might be removed; but his limbs refused to serve him, he was only dragged along, and those whose aid his father implored, seeing they could do no more, frankly declared that if they carried him they must themselves perish.

The unfortunate captain was driven to despair. Lifting his son on his shoulders, he tried to carry him; he could make but a single step, when he fell to the ground with his son who seemed more distressed with his father's grief than with his own sufferings. The heroic boy besought him to leave him to die; the sight, he said, of his father's tears and affliction were infinitely more severe than the bodily pain he endured. These words, far from inducing the captain to depart, melted him more and more, until he at last resolved to die with his son. The youth, astonished at his father's determination, and satisfied that his persuasions were unavailing, entreated the Portuguese in the most impressive manner to carry away his father.

Two priests who were of the party endeavored to represent to the captain the sinfulness of persisting in his resolution; but the Portuguese were obliged finally to carry him away by force, after having removed his son a little apart. So cruel, however, was the separation that the captain never recovered it. The violence of his grief was unabating; and he actually died of a broken heart after reaching the Cape.

"Manual labor to my father was not only good and decent for its own sake, but as he was given to saying, it straightened out one's thoughts."

MARY ELLEN CHASE

# Santa Claus

It has been said that men first believe in, then disbelieve in, then become—Santa Claus.

For children, Christmas Eve is almost impossibly exciting. Eventually they are persuaded into their beds, having prepared milk and cookies (ignoring their father's question, "Don't you think he would prefer whiskey?") and a short note asking for a Playstation, a small automobile, an entertainment system, Brad Pitt (batteries included), a Versace handbag, and so on.

You must wait, wait, wait, and wait. It is utter folly to doze, for you can guarantee that they'll be up before you on this one day of the year. So you wait until your partner is asleep, and then you make a trial run. You walk into the children's room: they're asleep.

And now an insane magic possesses you. You don The Garb: the ill-fitting Santa outfit that you foolishly bought on the cheap, which fits nowhere, and the beard that assaults the delicate nerve endings in your nostrils and ears. You begin to sweat. Why are you doing this?

You drink the milk, and hide the cookies in an almost inaccessible pocket. You hang the bulging stockings from the mantelpiece. You pick up the note, and replace it with one of your own, in cunningly disguised handwriting. They stir. You stand stock still. You feel like a thief in your own home.

They settle; you leave. They have not seen you.

They have not seen you. Why, then, have you dressed up? Why? Because there is a Santa Claus after all. And because in the morning you are woken with the beautiful, joyful yell, "He's been!"

# Father's Day

In many countries of the world, there is a special day to celebrate fatherhood, but it falls on many different days of the year. In Sweden, Norway, and Finland, it falls in November. In Australia and New Zealand, Father's Day is the first Sunday in September. In Brazil, it is on the second Sunday in August. In Germany, it is always celebrated on Ascension Day. Father's Day in the U.S., Canada, the U.K., France, Chile, and Japan, is celebrated on the third Sunday in June. In Lithuania it is the first Sunday in June. Many Catholics (in Spain and Spanish-speaking Latin America) honor their fathers on St. Joseph's Day, March 19, because Joseph was the father of Jesus.

In the U.S., Father's Day is widely thought to have been inaugurated by Mrs. Bruce John Dodd (also known as Sonora Louise Smart Dodd), whose father, a Civil War hero by the name of William Jackson Smart, had raised his six children on his own. Having heard a speech extolling motherhood and Mother's Day, she felt moved to urge the adoption of a Father's Day. In this, she was supported by local branches of the Ministerial Association and the Young Men's Christian Association, both of Spokane, Washington. The first national

Father's Day was on June 19, 1910, though it wasn't until 1972 that President Nixon signed it into law as a date of permanent national observance.

There are rival claims to the paternity of Father's Day: some say that it began with a church service in West Virginia in 1908, organized by a Mrs. Charles Clayton; others insist that the first Father's Day ceremony was held in Vancouver, Washington. The president of the Chicago branch of the Lions' Club, Harry Meek, is said to have celebrated the first Father's Day with his organization in 1915; the day chosen was the third Sunday in June because it was the closest date to Meek's own birthday! Meek once wrote a letter to the Frank Lyon Company encouraging the celebration of Meek Day: "I do modestly suggest that you and your employees should declare each anniversary of the date of this letter to be 'Meek Day', to be celebrated by feasting, fan dancing, and bullfights and things."

The truth of the matter, however, is that Father's Day has never really rivaled Mother's Day. In a recent survey, the second most popular gift for fathers on their special day was…nothing. This, at least, has the advantage of not being the soap on a rope vilified by Bill Cosby.

"None of you can ever be proud enough of being the child of such a father who has not his equal in this world—so great, so good, so faultless."

QUEEN VICTORIA

# Hopeless Dope!

Fathers can be most resourceful. Few occurrences are more embarrassing for a father than running out of gas—especially when the children are in the car—and having to call for his partner's assistance. There will follow an uncomfortable wait during which the children will have to be entertained.

The trick for the wise father is to make the best of a bad situation: instead of portraying himself as the victim of cruel circumstance, he should make himself out as a lovable, hopeless dope. The surprise of this revelation should ensure that the children are engulfed in shocked laughter for several minutes. Then, however, the hilarity will die down, and the children will stop repeating the highly comical phrase "hopeless dope" over and over again.

At that point the father must decide whether to turn Hopeless Dope into a character, around whom an adventure of unbelievable excitement may be woven. If he is a self-confident character, he will take this course. The self-confidence is needed because for the rest of his life he will be haunted by Hopeless Dope, and he will be asked on numerous occasions for further adventures. It is a big commitment, and it may be an easier course of action simply to open the hood and stare at the engine as though the trouble lay there, rather than in his own oafish mind.

# The Rigmarole of the Pipe

One summer his father took up a pipe. In retrospect, it was probably an attempt to give up smoking cigarettes, but at the time his son found it immensely exciting. He grew the beginnings of a beard to go with the pipe, and for a season this was a slightly different father, with a new smell, a new look. His son thought he looked like Ernest Hemingway, especially when he wore the heavy fisherman's sweater on colder days.

The rigmarole attached to pipe-smoking was especially intriguing. There was the sweet-smelling tobacco pouch, containing a slice of apple; there was the instrument itself: plain but with a beautiful bowl and fluted spout, in walnut, the mouthpiece in ebony. There were the multicolored pipe cleaners, with which the boy fashioned unconvincing animals.

"It's a giraffe."

"Oh."

There was the fishlike tamping knife, with its lovely scaled surface. There was the constant lighting of the tobacco, as it continually failed to ignite properly; there was the clamping of the teeth, and the suggestion of spittle at the lips; there was the delicious aroma that floated through the night air.

All this added to the father's mystery, the more so because it all disappeared as suddenly as it had come. He returned to his pipeless, beardless self. Nothing was lost, but there lingered the suggestion that he may, in some part of himself, have wanted to be other than how he was.

# Father William

LEWIS CARROLL

"You are old, Father William," the young man said,
"And your hair has become very white;
And yet you incessantly stand on your head –
Do you think, at your age, it is right?"

"In my youth," Father William replied to his son,
"I feared it might injure the brain;
But, now that I'm perfectly sure I have none,
Why, I do it again and again."

"You are old," said the youth, "as I mentioned before,
And have grown most uncommonly fat;
Yet you turned a back-somersault in at the door –
Pray, what is the reason of that?"

"In my youth," said the sage, as he shook his grey locks,
"I kept all my limbs very supple
By the use of this ointment – one shilling the box –
Allow me to sell you a couple?"

"You are old," said the youth, "and your jaws are too weak
For anything tougher than suet;
Yet you finished the goose, with the bones and the beak –
Pray, how did you manage to do it?"

"In my youth," said his father, "I took to the law,
And argued each case with my wife;
And the muscular strength which it gave to my jaw
Has lasted the rest of my life."

"You are old," said the youth, "one would hardly suppose
That your eye was as steady as ever;
Yet you balanced an eel on the end of your nose
What made you so awfully clever?"

"I have answered three questions, and that is enough,"
Said his father. "Don't give yourself airs!
Do you think I can listen all day to such stuff?
Be off, or I'll kick you downstairs!"

# Dads Behaving Badly

Once they reach a certain age (or rather once all their children have attained the age of eighteen), fathers become idiosyncratic, for they have been on their best behavior for about twenty years and now intend to revert to their former irresponsible selves.

They have provided the security and comfort required for their children to develop into idealistic, horribly enviable young adults, responsible for themselves. Now the fathers decide to grow beards, take up pipe-smoking, drink Jack Daniel's, and feel no compunction about passing sarcastic remarks about the socks their children have given them as their usual birthday present. They take up deplorable political positions without embarrassment. They wish to melt the Antarctic, cut down the rainforest, abolish all monarchies everywhere, ban Germans from motor-racing, and exclude Australians from Olympic swimming events.

They refuse to eat certain kinds of food, such as potatoes and pasta. "I've had enough starch in the last twenty years to keep me upright for a century," they might say mysteriously. They give up shouting at the TV, but this is only because they have ceased to watch it, and now shout at the radio or the newspaper. They like to make bonfires.

When the adult child is confronted by such a father, he should do absolutely nothing. It will soon become clear whether it is all a joke or whether the father has genuinely started a second adolescence (he has). Now the child can himself begin to look forward to the honesty that comes with age.

"Father and son in the kitchen is a recipe for disaster."

ANONYMOUS

# Plus Ça Change

"*Let me not close this paper without making an appeal to parents to instruct their young people in moral self-control…Too much license is allowed to children nowadays. This is doubtless a time for the young in a way that was unknown in the stricter period in which many of us were brought up, and while much of the stern repression of the children of the old days can be left to the bygone times, yet education in the control of selfish desires and passions is necessary even in the youngest children if we would see them happy and ready to fit into their environment.*"

from *What Fathers Should Tell Their Sons*, British Social Hygiene Council, 1925

Left: cover of *L'Histoire d'Alsace racontée aux petits enfants par l'Oncle Hansi*, illustrated by Jean-Jacques Hansi

# Family Feud

Her brother and father were in the garden, having a terrible argument. She sat on the steps of the house, watching and listening, distractedly picking needles off the rosemary bush. She couldn't move. She wanted to move, but their anger was mesmerizing.

Then her brother left, hurling an insult as he went. Her father hurled a flowerpot in return, which smashed against the gatepost. She didn't believe he meant to score a direct hit on her brother. Her brother walked away, ignoring the attack. Her father pursued him. They turned to face each other. More words were exchanged. Her father hit her brother; her brother pushed her father. Her brother walked off again. Her father returned to the house. He said, "I was in the army by the time I was nineteen, for Christ's sake." And then he paused. He looked at her. He said, "Well, no, actually I wasn't in the army by the time I was nineteen," and having said that to her he seemed relieved, and in his face she could see forgiveness replacing anger.

She said, "You and I never fight like that."

He said, "No. It's because I expect too much of him."

She said, "He's good, though. A good person."

Her father said, "Oh, I know that. I know I shouldn't have been angry. I should know better. I behaved badly. I shall have to apologize."

"It's because you care," she said. "He'll be sorry too."

She offered him a sprig of rosemary. He took it, sniffed, and smiled at her; she smiled back.

# Be Kind

MARGARET COURTNEY

*Be kind to thy father—for when*
*thou wert young,*

*Who loved thee so fondly as he?*

*He caught the first accents that fell*
*from thy tongue,*

*And joined in thine innocent glee.*

# A Different You

The death of your father will give you, eventually, a picture of him other than the one you have been used to as a child. What will always remain is the image of him as someone capable of putting a smile on a seemingly inconsolable face, and of holding you spellbound with tales (true or otherwise) of his adventures as a tyke. While the affection will not perish, the knowledge you have of him will increase now that he is finite, now that no more experience will touch him. You will begin to explore territory that is not simply uncharted, but undreamt of—you will be a kind of Christopher Columbus.

You will find (and you do not expect this) that your father lived a life without you in it. For this to be a discovery sounds absurd, because he gave you the benefit of his youthful experience, and related stories of his life that predated your appearance in it. You had assumed, without really knowing it, that all this experience, all these stories, had been garnered for your benefit, and that your father's life had been lived in preparation for yours. Now you find that this was not so. Perhaps you find, in old letters, or through a phone call, that he very nearly married a girl he met on holiday, and you realize how very different a "you" you might have been.

# Fun Project: 3

## MAKE A SPACE ROCKET

**MATERIALS**

Large gray or white cardboard box,
   big enough to sit in
2 cardboard tubes
Thin card, about 20-in/50-cm square
Corrugated cardboard, about
   $3\frac{1}{4}$ x 12in/8 x 30cm
Tissue or cellophane
   (yellow, red,
   orange)
Paints
Paintbrushes
Stickers
Color markers
Packing tape
Clear tape
String
Yarn needle
Scissors

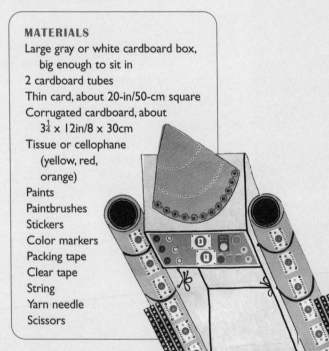

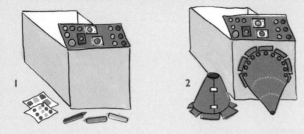

**1** Cut 3 flaps off the box, leaving the front flap for the control panel. Use stickers and color markers to make buttons and dials on the control panel.

**2** Cut one small and one large semicircle from thin card. Tape each into a cone shape. Cut the point off the small cone. Cut notches around the bottom of the cones and fold back. Tape the large cone to the front of the box, and the small cone to the back.

**3** Paint the tubes to look like boosters. Loop string around the front of each tube, thread through 2 holes in the side of the box, and tie on the inside. Make another loop for the back of each tube.

**4** Paint the corrugated cardboard side fins. Glue a fin onto each booster. Tape or glue strips of tissue or cellophane into the boosters and tail of the rocket to look like flames.

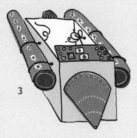

"Children can be useful: at least you don't need an alarm clock in the morning."

# The Railway Children

*by*

E. NESBIT

Only three people got out of the 11.54. The first was a countryman with two baskety boxes full of live chickens who stuck their russet heads out anxiously through the wicker bars; the second was Miss Peckitt, the grocer's wife's cousin, with a tin box and three brown-paper parcels; and the third –

"Oh! my Daddy, my Daddy!" That scream went like a knife into the heart of everyone in the train, and people put their heads out of the windows to see a tall pale man with lips set in a thin close line, and a little girl clinging to him with arms and legs, while his arms went tightly round her.

"I knew something wonderful was going to happen," said Bobbie, as they went up the road, "but I didn't think it was going to be this. Oh, my Daddy, my Daddy!"

"Then didn't Mother get my letter?" Father asked.

"There weren't any letters this morning. Oh! Daddy! it is really you, isn't it?"

The clasp of a hand she had not forgotten assured her that it was. "You must go in by yourself, Bobbie, and tell Mother quite quietly that it's all right. They've caught the man who did it. Everyone knows now that it wasn't your Daddy."

"I always knew it wasn't," said Bobbie. "Me and Mother and our old gentleman."

"Yes," he said, "it's all his doing. Mother wrote and told me you had found out. And she told me what you'd been to her. My own little girl!" They stopped a minute then.

And now I see them crossing the field. Bobbie goes into the house, trying to keep her eyes from speaking before her lips have found the right words to "tell Mother quite quietly" that the sorrow and the struggle and the parting are over and done, and that Father has come home.

I see Father walking in the garden, waiting – waiting. He is looking at the flowers, and each flower is a miracle to eyes that all these months of Spring and Summer have seen only flagstones and gravel and a little grudging grass. But his eyes keep turning towards the house. And presently he leaves the garden and goes to stand outside the nearest door. It is the back door, and across the yard the swallows are circling. They are getting ready to fly away from cold winds and keen frost to the land where it is always summer. They are the same swallows that the children built the little clay nests for.

Now the house door opens. Bobbie's voice calls: –

"Come in, Daddy; come in!"

He goes in and the door is shut....At the end of the field, among the thin gold spikes of grass and the harebells and Gipsy roses and St. John's Wort, we may just take one last look, over our shoulders, at the white house where neither we nor anyone else is wanted now.

# TV's Doting and Dysfunctional Dads

In the 1950s, men came back from work to a perfect home, a peck on the cheek from their wife, and delighted screams from their loving children. This idyllic existence was typified by Robert Young in *Father Knows Best*, in which the father (rather than changing into a superhero costume) simply swaps his suit for a cardigan and a pair of slippers and subsequently sorts out the problems of the world. The children are called Princess, Bud, and Kitten. Not too much surly adolescent angst there, then.

In the 1957 sitcom *Leave It To Beaver*, the son (who regularly got himself into some kind of a fix) always benefits from his father's worldly advice at the end of the show.

*The Andy Griffith Show* in 1961 took things a step further, presenting a single father (although it has to be said that his son, played by Ron Howard, never presented any serious threat to parental authority).

The long-running series *The Waltons*, which began in 1972 and continues to be repeated, painted a rosy portrait of rural family life. At the head of the family is John Walton (played by Ralph Waite), a wise but human father who, together with his equally wise wife and parents, brings up seven decent children during the hard times of the 1930s Depression.

In the mid-1980s, *The Cosby Show* started. The comedian Bill Cosby played Cliff, a father of such consummate fatherliness that the comedian ended up becoming an expert on the subject: "If the new American father feels bewildered and even defeated, let him take comfort from the fact that whatever he does in any fathering situation has a fifty percent chance of being right."

John Goodman's character, Dan, in the 1980s show *Roseanne*, is a blue-collar parent who spends far too much time fighting three difficult kids and one horribly witty wife. He worries about money and loves beer.

Which brings us to Homer Simpson, and his words of wisdom: "To alcohol! The cause of—and solution to—all life's problems." He is perhaps the most famous fictional father of today, a god among fathers, whose imperfections have a kind of sublime wisdom. So, on meeting aliens he yells, "Please don't eat me! I have a wife and kids. Eat them!" When asked if he would like some professional help for his son, he responds, "What do we need a psychiatrist for? We know our kid is nuts." And of course Homer is always ready to provide considered parental advice: "Kids, you tried your best and you failed miserably. The lesson is, never try."

Isn't it great to have role models?

# Sunday Morning

Sunday morning belongs to the father. If he wakes to find a bright, sunny day, he may decide to take his children to church, leaving the mother to the whims of Morpheus, the Roman god of sleep. Attendance at church will be chiefly for the purpose of the lusty singing of familiar hymns. But before piety comes breakfast. And before breakfast comes music, preferably Haydn.

So the house fills with symphonic Haydn, and five minutes later with the peerless aroma of freshly brewed coffee. This combination is utterly compelling, even to the bed-loving teenager—the grungey son who was still awake in the early hours, plugged into headphones that vibrated his brain cells with insistent, incoherent lyrics; the Sleeping Beauty of a daughter who rarely sees a morning that is not blighted by the dark prospect of formal education.

Descending on the kitchen in various states of dress, they are confronted by blueberry pancakes, bacon, sausages, eggs, hash browns, and toast. Unlike other days of the week, when everyone grabs breakfast on the run, today the father provides all. The moaning about church can wait.

Late morning is devoted to reading the newspaper, relishing the aroma of the roast in the oven, and watching one's family pass this leisurely day in various endearing ways.

# Dad's Favorite Recipe: 2

## BLUEBERRY PANCAKES

### INGREDIENTS
$1\frac{1}{4}$ cups/150g all-
  purpose (plain)
  flour
$\frac{1}{2}$ tsp baking powder
$\frac{1}{2}$ tsp baking soda
  (bicarbonate of
  soda)
$\frac{1}{4}$ tsp salt
1 cup/250ml
  buttermilk
$\frac{3}{4}$ cup/185ml milk
1 tbsp sugar or honey
2 tbsp/25g butter,
  melted
$\frac{1}{2}$ tsp vanilla extract
$\frac{1}{2}$ cup/120g fresh
  blueberries
melted butter or
  vegetable oil, for
  frying
butter and maple
  syrup or honey,
  to serve

**1** In a bowl, combine the flour, baking powder, baking soda, and salt, and make a well in the middle.

**2** In another bowl, whisk together the buttermilk, about $\frac{1}{2}$ cup/125ml of the milk, the sugar or honey, melted butter, and vanilla extract. Pour into the well and, using a whisk or fork, stir gently until just combined with the dry mixture. If the batter is too thick, add a little more milk so that it can be poured. Do not overbeat—a few floury lumps do not matter. Gently fold in the blueberries.

**3** Heat a large frying pan over medium heat and brush with melted butter or vegetable oil. Drop the batter in small ladlefuls onto the hot surface and cook until the edges are set and the surface bubbles begin to break, about 1 minute.

**4** Turn each pancake and cook until just golden underneath, about 30 seconds longer. Serve hot with butter and maple syrup or honey.

# The Musical Education

Music is important to a man, whether it is the emancipation of dissonance and the wacky sounds of the Second Viennese school, or the nursery rhythms of contemporary hip hop, and it is a love that he hopes to pass on to his children one day.

In the first instance babies must be sung to, and it is necessary to have a number of suitable songs at the ready, such as:

> *I'm a rambler, I'm a gambler,*
> *I'm a long way from home.*
> *And if you don't like me*
> *Then leave me alone.*
> *I eat when I'm hungry,*
> *I drink when I'm dry,*
> *And if moonshine don't kill me,*
> *I'll live till I die.*

The important thing is that songs should be memorable. Progress to spirituals, lilting reggae, calypso sounds, or gentle Mozart piano sonatas. It is not until around the age of ten that a child begins to be vulnerable to competing tastes in music. At this point it is important to strike firmly with a strategy to persuade the child to like the right music—in other words the music you like.

The options boil down to two: bombard the child with music you don't like, in order to make her rebel in favor of the music you do like, or bombard her with music you do like and hope she cannot fend off the onslaught. In reality, of course, it is difficult to make your child listen to music she doesn't like (although she will almost certainly make you listen, albeit unintentionally, to music you don't like.)

To win your campaign, expose your child to lots of different kinds of music. Compile an eclectic CD for the car that contains, for example, a chorus from the Bach B-minor mass, your favorite Vivaldi, the Mozart clarinet concerto (second movement), a few Wagner snippets, a short burst of Alban Berg, Elvis Presley singing "Mystery Train," three tracks from *Revolver* by the Beatles, something from Nirvana's *Nevermind*, an obscenity-free rap by Eminem (should such a thing exist), a Philip Glass composition, a chant by Bulgarian milkmaids, and a whistling Peruvian shepherd or two. Oh and don't forget that all-essential country track (though perhaps not Hank Williams singing "My Son Calls Another Man Daddy"). The child will be confused, and not know which music to revolt against. Half the battle will have been won.

RICHARD WAGNER AS A YOUNG BOY,
PLAYING THE PIANO FOR HIS PARENTS

# Daddy's Little Girl

Brothers can only look and wonder at the licence their sisters enjoy from their fathers. In the eyes of sons, fathers have a tendency to give daughters anything they could possibly wish for, and to forgive them even the most brutal misdemeanor.

For example, let us say that a child has been given an automobile, and let us say that this child has severely damaged its rear paneling by foolishly reversing into a fire hydrant. Whose fault is it? The answer depends entirely on the sex of the child. If it is male, the child is undoubtedly wholly at fault; he did not take sufficient care, and will be made to work to pay off the cost of repair. If the child is female, however, the father's reaction is to criticize the wholly inappropriate siting of the fire hydrant, and a letter might even be written to the appropriate department of the city government, with a veiled threat of legal proceedings should such a thing happen again.

The father loves his children equally, but the father knows his son as he does not know his daughter. There is no Adam in her, no sin; and where there is no sin, there is only virtue. It is wondrous to a father that he has contributed to the making of such purity, and his love for his daughter glows, and she will love him as she loves the sun, until the end of her life.

Dance to your daddy
My little babby
Dance to your daddy,
my little lamb.

You shall have a fishy
On a little dishy
You shall have a fishy
when the boat comes in.

# His Pride and Joy

She remembered him well, although he had died when she was six years old. She let the world know how she had loved him, and in that way he remained alive. She recalled riding on his shoulders as he took her to his favorite bar, a place where everyone knew and petted her. She was given cool lemonade; her father would drink a beer. He was a popular man, respected for the care and love he lavished on his daughter.

Occasionally, his wild temper gave rise to erratic acts. Once he had hurled a joint of lamb through the window: she loved that memory as vividly as she recalled her terror at his anger.

He had been a mechanic who loved to read. She loved him so much that she made great claims for him as an inventor. Nothing could dislodge her worship and her pride in his abilities. She had all his stories inside her head, the stories he told as he walked her about the town.

She often thought of her father as she waved her own daughter and husband off to their local bar, the very same one that had been her father's favorite.

# A Little Princess

*by*

FRANCES HODGSON BURNETT

Sara stood near her father and listened while he and Miss
Minchin talked. She had been brought to the seminary because
Lady Meredith's two little girls had been educated there, and
Captain Crewe had a great respect for Lady Meredith's
experience. Sara was to be what was known as "a parlor
boarder," and she was to enjoy even greater privileges than
parlor boarders usually did. She was to have a pretty bedroom
and sitting room of her own; she was to have a pony and a
carriage, and a maid to take the place of the ayah who had
been her nurse in India.

"I am not in the least anxious about her education," Captain
Crewe said, with his gay laugh, as he held Sara's hand and
patted it. "The difficulty will be to keep her from learning too
fast and too much. She is always sitting with her little nose
burrowing into books. She doesn't read them, Miss Minchin;
she gobbles them up as if she were a little wolf instead of a
little girl. She is always starving for new books to gobble, and
she wants grown-up books—great, big, fat ones—French and
German as well as English—history and biography and poets,
and all sorts of things. Drag her away from her books when ☞

she reads too much. Make her ride her pony in the Row or go out and buy a new doll. She ought to play more with dolls."

"Papa," said Sara, "you see, if I went out and bought a new doll every few days I should have more than I could be fond of. Dolls ought to be intimate friends. Emily is going to be my intimate friend."

Captain Crewe looked at Miss Minchin and Miss Minchin looked at Captain Crewe.

"Who is Emily?" she inquired.

"Tell her, Sara," Captain Crewe said, smiling.

Sara's green-gray eyes looked very solemn and quite soft as she answered.

"She is a doll I haven't got yet," she said. "She is a doll papa is going to buy for me. We are going out together to find her. I have called her Emily. She is going to be my friend when papa is gone. I want her to talk to about him."

Miss Minchin's large, fishy smile became very flattering indeed.

"What an original child!" she said. "What a darling little creature!"

"Yes," said Captain Crewe, drawing Sara close. "She is a darling little creature. Take great care of her for me, Miss Minchin."

Sara stayed with her father at his hotel for several days; in fact, she remained with him until he sailed away again to India. They went out and visited many big shops together, and bought a great many things. They bought, indeed, a great many more things than Sara needed; but Captain Crewe was a rash, innocent young man and wanted his little girl to have everything she admired and everything he admired himself, so between them they collected a wardrobe much too grand for a child of seven. There were velvet dresses trimmed with costly furs, and lace dresses, and embroidered ones, and hats with great, soft ostrich feathers, and ermine coats and muffs, and boxes of tiny gloves and handkerchiefs and silk stockings in such abundant supplies that the polite young women behind the counters whispered to each other that the odd little girl with the big, solemn eyes must be at least some foreign princess—perhaps the little daughter of an Indian rajah.

And at last they found Emily, but they went to a number of toy shops and looked at a great many dolls before they discovered her.

"I want her to look as if she wasn't a doll really," Sara said. "I want her to look as if she listens when I talk to her. The trouble with dolls, papa"—and she put her head on one side and reflected as she said it—"the trouble with dolls is that they never seem to hear." So they looked at big ones and little ones—at dolls with black eyes and dolls with blue—at dolls with brown curls and dolls with golden braids, dolls dressed and dolls undressed.

"You see," Sara said when they were examining one who had no clothes. "If, when I find her, she has no frocks, we can take her to a dressmaker and have her things made to fit. ☞

☞ They will fit better if they are tried on."

After a number of disappointments they decided to walk and look in at the shop windows and let the cab follow them. They had passed two or three places without even going in, when, as they were approaching a shop which was really not a very large one, Sara suddenly started and clutched her father's arm.

"Oh, papa!" she cried. "There is Emily!"

A flush had risen to her face and there was an expression in her green-gray eyes as if she had just recognized someone she was intimate with and fond of.

"She is actually waiting there for us!" she said. "Let us go in to her."

"Dear me," said Captain Crewe, "I feel as if we ought to have someone to introduce us."

"You must introduce me and I will introduce you," said Sara. "But I knew her the minute I saw her—so perhaps she knew me, too."

Perhaps she had known her. She had certainly a very intelligent expression in her eyes when Sara took her in her arms. She was a large doll, but not too large to carry about easily; she had naturally curling golden-brown hair, which hung like a mantle about her, and her eyes were a deep, clear, gray-blue, with soft, thick eyelashes which were real eyelashes and not mere painted lines.

"Of course," said Sara, looking into her face as she held her on her knee, "of course papa, this is Emily."

So Emily was bought and actually taken to a children's outfitter's shop and measured for a wardrobe as grand as Sara's own. She had lace frocks, too, and velvet and muslin ones, and hats and coats and beautiful lace-trimmed underclothes, and gloves and handkerchiefs and furs.

"I should like her always to look as if she was a child with a good mother," said Sara. "I'm her mother, though I am going to make a companion of her."

Captain Crewe would really have enjoyed the shopping tremendously, but that a sad thought kept tugging at his heart. This all meant that he was going to be separated from his beloved, quaint little comrade.

He got out of his bed in the middle of that night and went and stood looking down at Sara, who lay asleep with Emily in her arms. Her black hair was spread out on the pillow and Emily's golden-brown hair mingled with it, both of them had lace-ruffled nightgowns, and both had long eyelashes which lay and curled up on their cheeks. Emily looked so like a real child that Captain Crewe felt glad she was there. He drew a big sigh and pulled his mustache with a boyish expression.

"Heigh-ho, little Sara!" he said to himself "I don't believe you know how much your daddy will miss you."

# Fascinating Father Facts

**1** U. S. Presidents who never had children: George Washington (known as the "Father of the Country"), James Madison, Andrew Jackson, James Polk, James Buchanan, and Warren Harding.

**2** Fathers are more likely to be employed, and to work longer hours, than men without dependant children.

**3** The average age of first-time fathers is just under twenty-seven.

**4** In 1995, 643,608 men became fathers in England and Wales: the youngest was thirteen; the oldest seventy-five. Three out of four British fathers have their first child before their thirtieth birthday. One baby in three is born to a man who is not married to the mother of his child.

**5** In the eighteenth century, Feodor Vassilyev from Shuya in Russia had sixty-nine children by his first wife. These included sixteen pairs of twins, seven sets of triplets, and four sets of quadruplets. Sixty-seven of the children survived infancy. We do not know how he fared with his second wife.

**6** 60 percent of fathers in a recent US poll said they share equally in child-rearing duties: only 19 percent of spouses agreed.

**7** Recent studies indicate that fathers who are actively involved in childcare help raise children who are more empathetic; societies where fathers are more involved have less male domination and antagonism between the sexes.

**a joke...** A father was trying to teach his young son the evils of alcohol.

He put one worm in a glass of water and another worm in a glass of whiskey. The worm in the water lived, while the one in the whiskey curled up and died.

"Son," said the father, "what does that show you?"

"Well, Dad, it shows that if you drink alcohol, you will not have worms."

**8** Professor Katherine Wynne-Edwards of Queen's University, Canada, found that expectant dads had higher levels of the female hormone estradiol, lower testosterone, and higher cortisol just before the birth of their child. Cortisol has been associated with bonding and also increases in mothers just before they give birth.

**9** Scary but true: according to a recent U.S. study, for each additional $10,000 in salary fathers earn, they spend 5 minutes less per day with their children.

**10** The most fertile men in Europe are neither Spanish, nor French, nor even Italian. The most fertile men in Europe are Finnish. Must be the long nights…

"If Mom says 'no,' she means it.
If Dad says 'no,' it means maybe."

JOSEPH, AGED 13

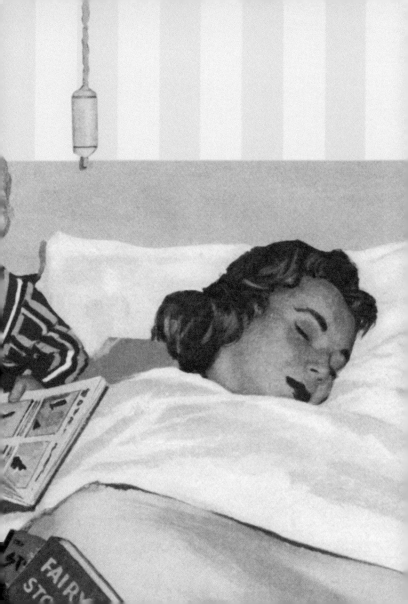

# Tough Love

*"It is impossible to please all the world and one's father."*

JEAN DE LA FONTAINE

She had never really performed well at school, in the academic sense. It had dispirited her, but her father had always staunchly supported her. Now, she was much more at home at drama school, learning how to act, how to perform on stage; she found she had a memory for the spoken word that she never possessed for the written word. She discovered that the math she favored was the geometry of movement.

She was to play Lady Macbeth in the final production of the year. Everyone recognized that the part should be hers. There was no jealousy among her fellow students. She was a generous girl, much liked. Her mother and father would be coming to the performance. She was looking forward to showing them what she could do, after the disappointments of her school career.

The show came off without a hitch. She loved the part, found it easy, and had few nerves. The applause at the final curtain was deafening. As she approached the front of the stage to take her solo bow, the entire audience rose. The ovation took her aback.

Afterwards she was surrounded by people congratulating her, promising great things for the years ahead. Finally her mother and father found their way through to her. Her mother hugged her with delight and excitement. She looked at her father. Her father patted her dismissively on the arm. "Easy money," he said, "easy money." Rarely had she felt so stung. She found it hard to forgive him; it seemed so unnecessarily cruel.

Later, when she had children herself, she understood. His principle was that little was so good or so bad as it seemed, and that the effusive praise you give for difficult work must be balanced by the moderated praise you give to what is easy. It is not the result, but the effort that is important. It was too late to thank him, but then perhaps he wouldn't have regarded himself as deserving of thanks.

EXTRACT FROM

# The Life of Charlotte Brontë

*by*

ELIZABETH GASKELL

[Charlotte] went into [her father's] study one afternoon after
his early dinner, carrying with her a copy of [*Jane Eyre*],
and one or two reviews, taking care to include a notice
adverse to it....

"Papa, I've been writing a book."

"Have you, my dear?"

"Yes, and I want you to read it."

"I am afraid it will try my eyes too much."

"But it is not in manuscript: it is printed."

"My dear! you've never thought of the expense it will be! It
will be almost sure to be a loss, for how can you get a book
sold? No one knows you or your name."

"But, papa, I don't think it will be a loss; no more will you,
if you will just let me read you a review or two, and tell you
more about it."

So she sat down and read some of the reviews to her father;
and then, giving him the copy of *Jane Eyre* that she intended
for him, she left him to read it. When he came in to tea, he
said, "Girls, do you know Charlotte has been writing a book,
and it is much better than likely?"

# Fun Project: 4

## MAKE A MINIATURE THEATER

### MATERIALS

Cardboard box, lid flaps
    cut off
Thin card, 2 pieces
    slightly smaller than
    the back of
    the box
4 lids or blocks, at least
    $1\frac{1}{4}$–in/3-cm deep
Color markers
Gold or silver marker
    pen
Paints
Paintbrushes
Gold star stickers
Gold or aluminum foil
Fabric scraps
2 garden canes
Clear tape
Scissors
Glue

**1** Cut a rectangle out of one side of the cardboard box for a stage opening (copy the picture above right for the correct position).

**2** Cut two V-shaped notches in the top of each side of the stage opposite each other. For the feet, glue a lid or block under each corner.

**3** Paint the walls and floor of the theater green. Paint the back wall dark blue, to make a night sky. Stick on star stickers and a foil moon.

**4** Paint the outside of the box red and the stage opening border purple. Above the stage add a gold foil crown and detail with gold pen.

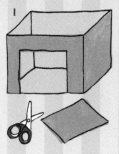

1

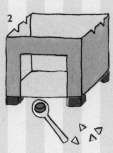

2

3

**5** Glue on fabric drapes then glue on small fabric tie-backs to keep them open.

**6** Draw or paint 2 scenes on the card. Glue or tape each scene to a garden cane. The canes rest on the notches cut in the sides of the box.

4

5

6

# CLOTHES PIN ACTORS

## MATERIALS

For the King, Fairy,
    Woman, and Wolf
4 old-fashioned wooden
    clothes pins
8 magnets
4 wooden spoons
Paints
Paintbrushes
Yellow tissue paper, thin strips
Yarn scraps (brown, yellow,
    orange)
Color markers
Fabric or felt scraps
Braid, sequins, star stickers
Brown paper, foil, thin card,
    scraps
Matchstick
Embroidery floss needle
Hacksaw (only to be used by
    an adult)
String
Scissors
Glue

**1** Ask an adult to saw each pin in half, just above where it splits into 2. Glue a magnet to the base of the top half.

**2** For people, draw or paint faces and bodies on the pins. Glue on yarn or tissue for hair, and braid or sequins as decoration. Glue or tie on a fabric cloak or dress. For a drawstring, gather the long edge of a rectangle of fabric using an embroidery needle and floss, ease the gathers around the neck and tie the thread ends in a bow. The Fairy's matchstick wand should have 2 sticker stars glued on back-to-back. For the King, glue on a yarn beard, a foil crown, and a fabric cloak fastened with a sequin.

**3** For the wolf, paint the pin brown. Draw its eyes, nose and mouth with a color marker. Glue on brown paper ears, wisps of yarn for hair and whiskers, and long strands for a tail. Glued-on bits of unraveled string give the Wolf's coat a coarser texture.

**4** Glue a magnet on each spoon. Make sure it is the correct way up to attract the magnet on its pin character. Decorate the handles with a color marker.

Use the long handled wooden spoons to move the actors on and off stage.

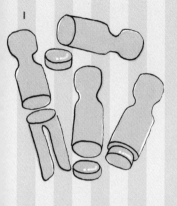

1

3

2

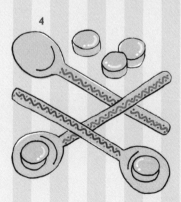

4

# Lock up Your Daughters

If you are on a cruise ship and your fifteen-year-old daughter (beautiful, self-assured, a tease) is attracting flocks of greasy-haired, over-indulged fifteen-year-old boys with florid cheeks and eager eyes, you can lock her in her cabin, no problem. On land, the problem is not so easily dealt with. Try to avoid confrontations, and keep the lines of communication open by paying as much attention as you possibly can to anything at all she says to you. (Also, it is important to intervene when daughter and mother are rolling around on the bedroom floor, each declaring that the other is ruining her life.)

For a fifteen-year-old girl, life can be ruined by major upsets such as Not Having Enough Money To Buy A Skirt or—and this is something that can take her to the edge of a breakdown—Parents Coming Home From The Theater Too Early. If either of these scenarios arises, prepare to be vilified as the most uncaring and inconsiderate father ever to have walked the earth.

Fifteen-year-old boys are, on the whole, easier than fifteen-year-old girls. This is because they don't talk as much. Some of them don't talk at all. Fifteen-year-old girls talk all the time.

The only way to silence them is to tell them that their makeup is running, or that their current pin-up has announced that he is either getting married or is gay. This news will gain you about twenty seconds' respite, but is invariably followed by a longer period of howling and ranting on the unfairness of life. Expect to hear the unanswerable question, "But why, daddy, why?"

Fathers sometimes feel that their most valid role (in their daughter's eyes) is as the unpaid chauffeur dedicated to facilitating a burgeoning social life. The fact is, you're doomed to picking her up whenever she wants, from wherever she wants. And you will be resigned to serving her in every possible way in order to save her from falling into the clutches of the evil little sprouts who come courting. The fact that she has no intention whatsoever of falling into such hands doesn't matter, because you know exactly what those evil little sprouts want, and it is very hard to see past that. But remember that your daughter has plenty of good sense. One day she'll marry, and you'll find it astonishing (as a wag once wittily observed) how someone so unworthy of your daughter's hand can father such perfect grandchildren.

"The sight that brings the deepest pride
to a father's heart is his children
proud of themselves."

ROSE O'KELLY

# Golden Bells

PO CHU I

When I was almost forty
I had a daughter whose name was Golden Bells.
Now it is just a year since she was born;
She is learning to sit and cannot yet talk.
Ashamed,—to find that I have not a sage's heart:
I cannot resist vulgar thoughts and feelings.
Henceforward I am tied to things outside myself:
My only reward,—the pleasure I am getting now.
If I am spared the grief of her dying young,
Then I shall have the trouble of getting her married.
My plan for retiring and going back to the hills
Must now be postponed for fifteen years!

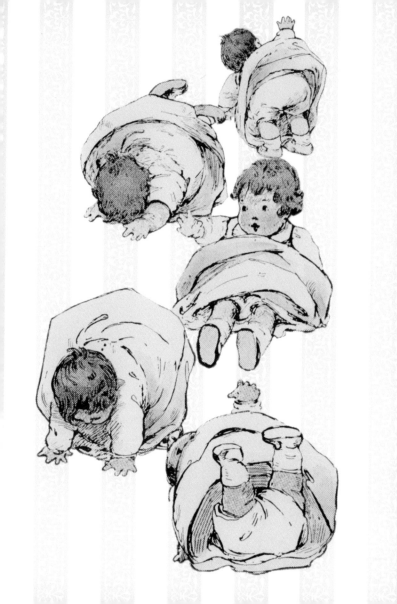

# Giving Your Daughter Away

Traditionally, it is the responsibility of the parents of the bride to pay for a wedding. However, the father of the bride will have almost no input into the wedding arrangements whatsoever, however hard he tries to intervene. All (all?) he has to do is to give his daughter away to the accountant/jazz drummer/skateboard champion with whom she has chosen to spend the rest of her life.

The way this is done is as follows: father and daughter turn up at the church some five minutes late. They pose for too many photographs. A bridesmaid spreads the bride's train. Inside, the organ starts, slow and solemn. The daughter takes her father's arm. He puts his hand on her hand, in a kind of clasp that is supposed to communicate calm, but which really means, "No! You're mine!" They proceed up the nave of the church, everyone smiling like crazy, and the father cannot take in what is happening to him. He is about to give his daughter away! As though that were what he wanted to do! The father and daughter stand to the left of the bridegroom, and the bride's hand falls from her father's arm. The final awful moment comes when the clergyman asks, "Who giveth this woman?" and incredibly the father takes his daughter's hand and passes it to the clergyman. He is suddenly no longer the most important man in his daughter's life.

And so the formal life of the father comes to an end. He has no public duties left to perform, and can settle into the business of becoming wise and old and, God willing, grandfatherly.

# Pride and Prejudice

*by*

JANE AUSTEN

Mr. Collins was not left long to the silent contemplation of his successful love; for Mrs. Bennet, having dawdled about in the vestibule to watch for the end of the conference, no sooner saw Elizabeth open the door and with quick step pass her towards the staircase, than she entered the breakfast room, and congratulated both him and herself in warm terms on the happy prospect of their nearer connection. Mr. Collins received and returned these felicitations with equal pleasure, and then proceeded to relate the particulars of their interview, with the result of which he trusted he had every reason to be satisfied, since the refusal which his cousin had steadfastly given him would naturally flow from her bashful modesty and the genuine delicacy of her character.

This information, however, startled Mrs. Bennet; – she would have been glad to be equally satisfied that her daughter had meant to encourage him by protesting against his proposals, but she dared not to believe it, and could not help saying so.

"But depend upon it, Mr. Collins," she added, "that ☞

Right: "And this offer of marriage you have refused?" by Charles Edmond Brock

Lizzy shall be brought to reason. I will speak to her about it myself directly. She is a very headstrong foolish girl, and does not know her own interest; but I will make her know it."

"Pardon me for interrupting you, Madam," cried Mr. Collins; "but if she is really headstrong and foolish, I know not whether she would altogether be a very desirable wife to a man in my situation, who naturally looks for happiness in the marriage state. If therefore she actually persists in rejecting my suit, perhaps it were better not to force her into accepting me, because if liable to such defects of temper, she could not contribute much to my felicity."

"Sir, you quite misunderstand me," said Mrs. Bennet, alarmed. "Lizzy is only headstrong in such matters as these. In every thing else she is as good natured a girl as ever lived. I will go directly to Mr. Bennet, and we shall very soon settle it with her, I am sure."

She would not give him time to reply, but hurrying instantly to her husband, called out as she entered the library,

"Oh! Mr. Bennet, you are wanted immediately; we are all in an uproar. You must come and make Lizzy marry Mr. Collins, for she vows she will not have him, and if you do not make haste he will change his mind and not have her."

Mr. Bennet raised his eyes from his book as she entered, and fixed them on her face with a calm unconcern which was not in the least altered by her communication.

"I have not the pleasure of understanding you," said he, when she had finished her speech. "Of what are you talking?"

"Of Mr. Collins and Lizzy. Lizzy declares she will not have Mr. Collins, and Mr. Collins begins to say that he will not have Lizzy."

"And what am I to do on the occasion? – It seems an hopeless business."

"Speak to Lizzy about it yourself. Tell her that you insist upon her marrying him."

"Let her be called down. She shall hear my opinion."

Mrs. Bennet rang the bell, and Miss Elizabeth was summoned to the library.

"Come here, child," cried her father as she appeared. "I have sent for you on an affair of importance. I understand that Mr. Collins has made you an offer of marriage. Is it true?" Elizabeth replied that it was. "Very well – and this offer of marriage you have refused?"

"I have, Sir."

"Very well. We now come to the point. Your mother insists upon your accepting it. Is not it so, Mrs. Bennet?"

"Yes, or I will never see her again."

"An unhappy alternative is before you, Elizabeth. From this day you must be a stranger to one of your parents. – Your mother will never see you again if you do not marry Mr. Collins, and I will never see you again if you do."

Elizabeth could not but smile at such a conclusion of such a beginning; but Mrs. Bennet, who had persuaded herself that her husband regarded the affair as she wished, was excessively disappointed.

"There are no days we enjoy so much as those shared with our father."

IONA ALLFORD

# Presidents and Patriarchs

*"My father taught me to work; he did not teach me to love it. I never did like to work, and I don't deny it. I'd rather read, tell stories, crack jokes, talk, laugh—anything but work."*
ABRAHAM LINCOLN

As a boy, John Adams was not keen on school. His teacher, a man called Cleverly, was one of the laziest men Adams ever recalled meeting, and Adams soon became fascinated with "idle pursuits" such as marbles and, later on, hunting. Adams' lack of interest in schooling and his father's intense desire to educate his son became a great bone of contention in the Adams household. The father prevailed; later John Adams became President of the U. S. His son, John Quincy Adams, also held this post. He began his political career with a trip to Russia as his father's secretary, when he was eighteen years old.

President Andrew Jackson's father died before he was born. President Abraham Lincoln never ever mentioned his father. President James Garfield's father died in a fire. President Calvin Coolidge always kissed his father hello and goodbye. President Ronald Reagan's father was a salesman, Democrat, and a fine storyteller to boot.

The only bachelor to hold the office of president was James Buchanan. Abraham Lincoln's son, Robert Todd Lincoln, was present at the assassination of three presidents: his father, James Garfield, and William McKinley. After the last shooting, he refused to attend any more State affairs. A couple of years before his father's assassination, Robert Lincoln's life was saved at a railroad station in New Jersey by a man called Edwin Booth; by a strange twist of fate, Abraham Lincoln's assassin was Edwin Booth's brother, John Wilkes Booth.

The father of the future President Theodore Roosevelt was a glass importer, and very wealthy. Nonetheless, he disapproved of the idea of a college education for his son, believing it would spoil him. The father was rich but infinitely charitable. It is said that he once arrived at a meeting of important New York dignitaries, to discuss matters of the gravest concern to the city, with a stray kitten in his pocket. According to his son, he was "the finest man I ever knew, and the happiest."

Once President Roosevelt was in office, he allowed his children to roam wild in the White House. When a pompous secretary of state complained about his daughter Alice interrupting an important meeting, Roosevelt said, "I can be President of the United States or I can control Alice. I cannot possibly do both."

# Letters from Father,
## President of the U.S.A.

Teddy Roosevelt wrote many charming, humorous letters to his children while he was President, and gave a fascinating insight into the havoc they wreaked in the White House.

White House, Feb. 27, 1904

*Dear Kermit:*

*Mother went off for three days to New York and Mame and Quentin took instant advantage of her absence to fall sick. Quentin's sickness was surely due to a riot in candy and ice-cream with chocolate sauce. He was a very sad bunny next morning and spent a couple of days in bed. Ethel, as always, was as good as gold both to him and to Archie, and largely relieved me of my duties as vice-mother. I got up each morning in time to breakfast with Ethel and Archie before they started for school, and I read a certain amount to Quentin, but this was about all. I think Archie escaped with a minimum of washing for the three days. One day I asked him before Quentin how often he washed his face, whereupon Quentin interpolated, "very seldom, I fear," which naturally produced from Archie violent recriminations of a strongly personal type. Mother came back yesterday, having thoroughly enjoyed Parsifal. All the horses continue sick.*

*Dearest Archie:*

*Ethel has bought on trial an eight-months bulldog pup. He is very cunning, very friendly, and wriggles all over in a frantic desire to be petted.*

*Quentin really seems to be getting on pretty well with his baseball. In each of the last two games he made a base hit and a run. I have just had to give him and three of his associates a dressing down—one of the three being Charlie Taft. Yesterday afternoon was rainy, and four of them played five hours inside the White House. They were very boisterous and were all the time on the verge of mischief, and finally they made spit-balls and deliberately put them on the portraits. I did not discover it until after dinner, and then pulled Quentin out of bed and had him take them all off the portraits, and this morning required him to bring in the three other culprits before me. I explained to them that they had acted like boors; that it would have been a disgrace to have behaved so in any gentleman's house; that Quentin could have no friend to see him, and the other three could not come inside the White House, until I felt that a sufficient time had elapsed to serve as punishment. They were four very sheepish small boys when I got through with them.*

# Doting on Daughters

A spokesman for the Important International Organization had told the press that a statement would be read out at 10:00 a.m. The reputation of the organization rested on this statement. The chief executive had decided to compose it himself, and take full responsibility for it.

His life was complicated by the fact that his youngest daughter was in the hospital, where her mother was also staying in order to keep her company. Before working on the statement, he had to get the other two girls off to school. The girls set off; it was 8:00 a.m. He walked upstairs, sat down at his desk, and picked up a pen. (This all happened in the days before e-mails or computers; he would be dictating his statement.)

The doorbell rang. It was one of his daughters. She was crying inconsolably. On her way to the school bus, she had passed the lifeless body of the family cat. It had been run over.

The father comforted his daughter, and told her he would go and get the cat so they could bury it in the back garden. They did so, and stood for a moment by the grave.

The father decided that perhaps the best thing to do was to take his daughter to the hospital to be with her mother. By the time he returned home, it was well past 9:00 a.m.

He sat down at his desk. The phone rang. It was the press department, telling him that most of the journalists were there and wanting to know if the statement was ready.

"Not quite," said the chief executive, picking up his pen.

Suddenly, he heard a strange miaowing sound. He could not make out where the noise came from. It was repeated several times. Eventually, he stood up and opened the door of his study. Three tiny kittens had somehow ascended the staircase in search of their mother, in search of food. The chief executive looked down at the kittens; he looked back at his desk; he looked at the time. There was only one thing for it. He fetched the kittens a saucer of milk.

The phone rang. "The chairman is ready, sir. I'm putting your secretary on the line to take the dictation."

"Very well." The chief executive coughed once, said a short prayer and began to speak into the telephone.

The world never knew that he hadn't prepared a single word of the statement in advance; the reputation of the Important International Organization was saved.

His children were told that the moral of this story was that "life interferes," but they preferred to remember it as an example of their good father's kind heart.

THE TOY SHOP, BY FRANCIS DONKIN BEDFORD

# Uncle Tom's Cabin

*by*

HARRIET BEECHER STOWE

It was late in the afternoon, and the rays of the sun formed
a kind of glory behind [Eva], as she came forward in her
white dress, with her golden hair and glowing cheeks, her
eyes unnaturally bright with the slow fever that burned in
her veins.

St. Clare had called her to show a statuette that he had been
buying for her; but her appearance, as she came on, impressed
him suddenly and painfully. There is a kind of beauty so
intense, yet so fragile, that we cannot bear to look at it. Her
father folded her suddenly in his arms, and almost forgot what
he was going to tell her.

"Papa," said Eva, with sudden firmness "I've had things I
wanted to say to you, a great while. I want to say them now,
before I get weaker."

St. Clare trembled as Eva seated herself in his lap. She laid
her head on his bosom, and said,

"It's all no use, papa, to keep it to myself any longer. The
time is coming that I am going to leave you. I am going, and
never to come back!" and Eva sobbed.

"O, now, my dear little Eva!" said St. Clare, trembling as he spoke, but speaking cheerfully, "you've got nervous and low-spirited; you mustn't indulge such gloomy thoughts. See here, I've bought a statuette for you!"

"No, papa," said Eva, putting it gently away, "don't deceive yourself!—I am not any better, I know it perfectly well,—and I am going, before long. I am not nervous,—I am not low-spirited. If it were not for you, papa, and my friends, I should be perfectly happy. I want to go,—I long to go!"

"Why, dear child, what has made your poor little heart so sad? You have had everything, to make you happy, that could be given you."

"I had rather be in heaven; though, only for my friends' sake, I would be willing to live. There are a great many things here that make me sad, that seem dreadful to me; I had rather be there; but I don't want to leave you,—it almost breaks my heart!"

"What makes you sad, and seems dreadful, Eva?"

"O, things that are done, and done all the time. I feel sad for our poor people; they love me dearly, and they are all good and kind to me. I wish, papa, they were all free."

"Why, Eva, child, don't you think they are well enough off now?"

"O, but, papa, if anything should happen to you, what would become of them? There are very few men like you, papa. Uncle Alfred isn't like you, and mamma isn't; and then, think of poor old Prue's owners! What horrid things people do, and can do!" and Eva shuddered.

☞ "My dear child, you are too sensitive. I'm sorry I ever let you hear such stories."

"O, that's what troubles me, papa. You want me to live so happy, and never to have any pain,—never suffer anything,—not even hear a sad story, when other poor creatures have nothing but pain and sorrow, and their lives;—it seems selfish. I ought to know such things, I ought to feel about them! Such things always sunk into my heart; they went down deep; I've thought and thought about them. Papa, isn't there any way to have all slaves made free?"

"That's a difficult question, dearest. There's no doubt that this way is a very bad one; a great many people think so; I do myself. I heartily wish that there were not a slave in the land; but, then, I don't know what is to be done about it!"

"Papa, you are such a good man, and so noble, and kind, and you always have a way of saying things that is so pleasant, couldn't you go all round and try to persuade people to do right about this? When I am dead, papa, then you will think of me, and do it for my sake. I would do it, if I could."

"When you are dead, Eva," said St. Clare, passionately. "O, child, don't talk to me so! You are all I have on earth."

"Poor old Prue's child was all that she had,—and yet she had to hear it crying, and she couldn't help it! Papa, these poor creatures love their children as much as you do me. O! do something for them! There's poor Mammy loves her children; I've seen her cry when she talked about them. And Tom loves his children; and it's dreadful, papa, that such things are happening, all the time!"

"There, there, darling," said St. Clare, soothingly; "only don't distress yourself, don't talk of dying, and I will do anything you wish."

"And promise me, dear father, that Tom shall have his freedom as soon as"—she stopped, and said, in a hesitating tone— "I am gone!"

"Yes, dear, I will do anything in the world—anything you could ask me to."

"Dear papa," said the child, laying her burning cheek against his, "how I wish we could go together!"

"Where, dearest?" said St. Clare.

"To our Saviour's home; it's so sweet and peaceful there—it is all so loving there!" The child spoke unconsciously, as of a place where she had often been. "Don't you want to go, papa?" she said.

St. Clare drew her closer to him, but was silent.

"You will come to me," said the child, speaking in a voice of calm certainty which she often used unconsciously.

"I shall come after you. I shall not forget you."

The shadows of the solemn evening closed round them deeper and deeper, as St. Clare sat silently holding the little frail form to his bosom. …St. Clare saw and felt many things, but spoke nothing; and, as it grew darker, he took his child to her bed-room; and, when she was prepared for rest; he sent away the attendants, and rocked her in his arms, and sung to her till she was asleep.

# The Maker of Laughter

Frankly, babies can be a bit dull to begin with. They rob you of sleep, invade your bed, ruin your clothes, and take away from you the company of the most beautiful woman on earth—all of which tends to infuriate a new father. It is all the things that babies don't do that makes them dull; they're not even very good at passive stuff like watching TV. They don't understand soccer or the Marx brothers. They can't talk.

What the father is waiting for is laughter. He's not really that impressed by a smile or a gurgle because anyone can make the baby do that. No, the father is waiting to assume his true role in the life of his child: maker of laughter.

Once baby and father laugh together, they know they are on the same side. This may explain why, in survey after survey, women always say that what they look for in a man is not chiseled features, but a GSOH (good sense of humor).

Indeed, a GSOH is vital in the early years of parenthood. The father must do lots of things that may not come naturally to him: supporting the mother, cooking, being practical; he must occasionally go so far as to do a bit of laundry. He can make jokes about all this, but he must not fail to fulfill these roles, or he's going to be in trouble. But one day his efforts will be rewarded—he will try something in front of his child, and instead of a gurgle acknowledging attention, the eyebrows will rise in just the right kind of way, and his child, by God, will laugh.

# Wait Till Your Dad Gets Home!

It used to be the case that mothers could threaten their children with a kind of doomsday weapon—that of "Wait until your dad gets home." This worked because the father was altogether less familiar to his children than the mother, and therefore less vulnerable to the ravaging power of contempt.

Nowadays, mothers and fathers often spend equal amounts of time with their children, and there is no doomsday weapon. What is more, in families where the mother is the breadwinner, you are very unlikely to hear the words "Wait until your mother gets home," because unfortunately, working mothers often feel more guilty about not being with their children than do working fathers.

The working mother is more likely to return home laden with computer games and DVDs than to return bristling with strong authority. She is no less exhausted by her day's work than any man, a state which brings irritation and shortness of temper, but her children will know that she feels guilty (children know everything about you they need to know) even as she explains to them, "I've been working all day to put food in your mouths."

The modern father, then, does not have the power of old, and must find new ways of disciplining his children. Unfortunately, fathers being men, the solution is usually to allow just about everything. That way your children cannot be naughty; so they need not be punished. Hence, good children. Simple, really.

# The Spanish Tragedy

*by*

THOMAS KYD

My son? And what's a son? A thing begot

Within a pair of minutes, thereabout;

A lump bred up in darkness, and doth serve

To balance those light creatures we call women,

And at nine months' end creeps forth to light.

What is there yet in a son to make a father

Dote, rave or run mad? Being born, it pouts,

Cries, and breeds teeth. What is there yet in a son?

He must be fed, be taught to go and speak.

Ay, and yet? Why might not a man love

A calf as well, or melt in passion over

A frisking kid, as for a son? Me thinks

A young bacon or a fine smooth little horse-colt

Should move a man as much as doth a son;

For one of these in very little time

Will grow to some good use, whereas a son,

The more he grows in stature and in years,

The more unsquar'd, unbevell'd he appears,

Reckons his parents among the rank of fools,

Strikes cares upon their heads with his mad riots,

Makes them look old before they meet with age.

This is a son! And what a loss were this,

Considered truly! Oh, but my Horatio

Grew out of reach of those insatiate humours:

He lov'd his loving parents, he was my comfort

And his mother's joy, the very arm that did

Hold up our house, our hopes were stored up in him.

# Don't Forget Mom's Birthday

It was the day before her mom's birthday, and she hadn't bought her a gift. Her father was furious, and when he was furious it was as if the earth trembled. He was like King Lear in his fury.

In the morning, her father gave her money to try to buy a gift on the way to or from school. He was still angry. Days before, he had asked her to buy her mother something, and she had failed. She went to school miserable and guilty.

Her father arranged to take her mother for a birthday lunch at a grand restaurant. Her mother was surprised, pleased, and girlishly flattered; she couldn't help herself. But when the father told her that they would have a surprise guest, she was disappointed, really disappointed. She didn't want a surprise guest. This was her birthday. The father promised she wouldn't mind this surprise guest. She couldn't think of anyone at all who wouldn't disappoint her. She had been so enjoying this occasion, and now, well…

At the end of the morning lessons, the daughter was summoned to the school office. Someone was waiting for her: it was her uncle. They drove to town, to the grand restaurant. She was the surprise guest. Her mother beamed with love. The daughter sat and ate scallops, and knew that her father had forgiven her for her thoughtlessness, and forgiven himself for his anger.

After lunch her father and mother took her back to school. The daughter always remembered this birthday as though it had been her own.

# Loving Kindness

It has been said that the most important thing a father can do for his children is to love their mother. This "love" should not be of the fickle, romantic kind, but rather of the lasting, cherished kind—in other words a giving, not selfish love.

After a child, particularly the first child, is born there is an enormous shift in sensibility. A family has been born. Affection, time, and concern must now be divided between partner and child. The mother will undoubtedly be consumed by the baby. She has, initially at least, little time for her spouse whose role is now solely as father. He is both wanted and needed. For his part, he feels an unexpected surge of love for his child, for he had thought that he couldn't possibly have any more love to give. He also has an overwhelming desire to protect that which he has helped to make and for the first time in his life, he feels truly important (which may make up for the fact that he won't be allowed to sleep in his own bed for a while.)

As time goes by, the parents will discover differences in each other which they could not have imagined. This will have nothing to do with the romantic affection they feel toward one another. That was merely what brought them together. They will disagree about aspects of child-rearing and will consequently have to bring the experiences of two utterly different lives into harmony. This is called loving kindness, and it is the antithesis of the romantic idea of love, for it is selfless and it is the higher love that children should be raised in.

Old Mother Goose became quite new,
And joined a woman's club;
She left poor Father Goose at home
To care for Sis and Bub.

They called for stories by the score,
And laughed and cried to hear
All of the queer and merry songs
That in this book appear.

When Mother Goose at last returned
For her there was no use;
The goslings much preferred to hear
The tales of Father Goose.

from *Father Goose: His Book* by L. Frank Baum,
illustration by W. W. Denslow

# Pampering Mother

Mother's Day, as all fathers, sons, and daughters know, is much more important than Father's Day. As the mother is often first to rise in the household, special arrangements have to be made to get up before her. The father must get out of bed without disturbing the maternal slumber, and then get the children up without waking the entire neighborhood with the growing whine that will issue from their little voiceboxes as protest against the inhumane treatment they are receiving.

Once he has managed to get the little angels into the kitchen, it may be that he will have to commission some rapid writing and drawing of Mother's Day cards that have negligently been left unwritten and undrawn until the last conceivable moment. He must then oversee the cooking of breakfast (a boiled egg is ideal, especially if one of the children has fashioned an egg-cosy for the occasion), and its safe delivery to the bedroom on a prettily appointed tray.

The father may find that he will have to boil another egg, the first having been timed by the son, and therefore either of a liquid consistency analogous to cold gravy or as hard as a pool ball. He will also have to make another cup of coffee, because the one his daughter made was strong enough to blow her mother's circuits. The father will not get credit for any of these things, for Mother's Day is of course characterized by extravagant praise of the children's thoughtfulness, care, and general all-round loveliness.

# Dad's Favorite Recipe: 3

## LITTLE CAKES FOR LITTLE KIDS

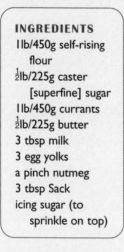

**INGREDIENTS**
1lb/450g self-rising
flour
½lb/225g caster
[superfine] sugar
1lb/450g currants
½lb/225g butter
3 tbsp milk
3 egg yolks
a pinch nutmeg
3 tbsp Sack
icing sugar (to
sprinkle on top)

This easy recipe is taken from *The Closet of Sir Kenelme Digby Opened*, by Sir Kenelme Sigby in 1669. The cakes are cute and the kids will have lots of fun following the quaint instructions!

"Take one pound of very fine flower, and put to it half a pound of sugar. Add one pound of currants well washed. When your flower is well mixed with the sugar and currants, you must put in it a half a pound of melted butter, three spoonfuls of milk, with the yolks of three new-laid eggs beat with it, some nutmeg; and if you please, three spoonfuls of Sack.

When you have mixed your paste well, you must put it in a dish by the fire, till it be warm. Then make them up in little cakes, and prick them full of holes. Bake them in a quick oven unclosed [200°C/400°F for 20 minutes]. Afterwards sprinkle them with sugar. The Cakes should be about the bigness of a hand-breadth and thin; of the cise of the Sugar Cakes sold at Barnet.

*Word List: flower = flour, cise = size, bigness = size, Sack = dry Spanish wine (can be left out or dry sherry used instead)"*

# Father of a Country

Men who achieve the status of "father of a country" fall into two distinct groups: scoundrels and genuine patriots, the former usually declaring their paternity themselves.

Roman emperors who received the honorific title *pater patriae* (father of his country) included Julius Caesar, Augustus, Hadrian, Diocletian, Marcus Aurelius, and Constantine the Great. On the other hand, the award was also granted to Caligula, Nero, and Commodus. (Commodus was the son of Marcus Aurelius, and he wanted to rename Rome after himself. Thankfully, he was strangled by a wrestler before he could do that, and so we do not have to refer to the Eternal City as Commodium.)

Similarly, more recent fathers of a country include George Washington (U. S.), Simón Bolívar (various South American countries), Thomas Masaryk (Czechoslovakia), Vaclav Havel (Czech Republic), Mohandas Gandhi (India), Kemal Atatürk (Turkey), David Ben-Gurion (Israel), and Nelson Mandela (South Africa).

The first recorded father of a country was not a leader at all, although he was indeed a politician—namely the Roman statesman, orator, and author, Cicero. (The name "Cicero" means "garbanzo bean," and stemmed from an ancestor who had a wart at the end of his nose that looked like a garbanzo bean.) Cicero was also a father, and indeed divorced his second wife Publilia because she showed insufficient grief at the death (in childbirth) of Tullia, Cicero's much-loved daughter from his first marriage.

When George Washington was young
And full of energy,
He took his little hatchet
And chopped a cherry tree.

His father grew quite angry,
This sorry sight to see,
For he was very fond indeed
Of that same cherry tree.

And so he questioned Georgie:
"Who did this thing?" said he.
"I cannot tell a lie," said George,
"I chopped the cherry tree!"

# Memoirs

*by*

CHARLES DARWIN

"Our poor child, Annie, was born in Gower Street, on March 2, 1841, and expired at Malvern at mid-day on the 23rd of April, 1851.

"I write these few pages, as I think in after years, if we live, the impressions now put down will recall more vividly her chief characteristics. From whatever point I look back at her, the main feature in her disposition which at once rises before me, is her buoyant joyousness, tempered by two other characteristics, namely, her sensitiveness, which might easily have been overlooked by a stranger, and her strong affection. Her joyousness and animal spirits radiated from her whole countenance, and rendered every movement elastic and full of life and vigour. It was delightful and cheerful to behold her. Her dear face now rises before me, as she used sometimes to come running downstairs with a stolen pinch of snuff for me her whole form radiant with the pleasure of giving pleasure. Even when playing with her cousins, when her joyousness almost passed into boisterousness, a single glance of my eye, not of displeasure (for I thank God I hardly ever cast one on her), but of want of sympathy, would for some minutes alter her whole countenance.

"The other point in her character, which made her joyousness and spirits so delightful, was her strong affection, which was of a most clinging, fondling nature. When quite a baby, this showed itself in never being easy without touching her mother, when in bed with her; and quite lately she would, when poorly, fondle for any length of time one of her mother's arms. When very unwell, her mother lying down beside her seemed to soothe her in a manner quite different from what it would have done to any of our other children.

So, again, she would at almost any time spend half an hour in arranging my hair, 'making it,' as she called it, 'beautiful,' or in smoothing, the poor dear darling, my collar or cuffs – in short, in fondling me.

"Beside her joyousness thus tempered, she was in her manners remarkably cordial, frank, open, straightforward, natural, and without any shade of reserve. Her whole mind was pure and transparent. One felt one knew her thoroughly and could trust her. I always thought, that come what might, we should have had in our old age at least one loving soul which nothing could have changed. All her movements were vigorous, active, and usually graceful. When going round the Sand-walk with me, although I walked fast, yet she often used to go before, pirouetting in the most elegant way, her dear face bright all the time with the sweetest smiles....

"We have lost the joy of the household, and the solace of our old age. She must have known how we loved her. Oh, that she could now know how deeply, how tenderly, we do still and shall ever love her dear joyous face! Blessings on her!"

# Four Generations

A father sits at a kitchen table. His son is agitatedly pacing the room, spitting out a stream of worries. He doesn't know how he's going to manage. He doesn't know enough about himself. He's not prepared. Pace, pace, pace. The fond father watches and remembers his own anxieties about impending fatherhood. If you have any sense of responsibility, it isn't easy to become a father. Thirty years on, it still isn't straightforward. How can he calm his son? How can he explain that in some sense, life looks after itself?

He remembers his own father, in a different lifetime, offering him advice when he was a conscientious young man who did not know what to think about a war being fought in a far-off place. "What can I do?" his younger self had asked, while hacking at a loaf of bread. His father had said, in his dry, detached tone, "You can learn how to cut a loaf of bread, for a start." At the time this had seemed a ludicrous, useless remark, but as the son who is now a father sits at the kitchen table, he remembers the loaf but he does not remember the causes of the war, or at least he cannot recall the angst that had gripped him. What his father had been saying, in his brusque way, was that one should attend to what can be attended to.

And so now, aware perhaps of his own fatuousness, he reaches across the kitchen table and pulls the breadboard towards him.

"Son."

"Dad?"

"There's an important thing I want you to know."

"What's that?"

"Come here." The boy goes to his father.

"This is how you cut a loaf of bread." Methodically and with theatrical care, the father cuts the loaf while the son stares, exasperated.

Fifteen years later the son watches the daughter that was born that night. She is cutting a loaf of bread. She seems angry about something, and she is ham-handed. He goes over to her and, taking the knife, holds the loaf firmly in place with his left hand and says, "This is how you cut a loaf of bread."

# Quality Time

Spending time with your children takes a number of forms. Mundane tasks such as chauffeuring invariably take up a lot of time, whether it is the school run, a lift to baseball practice, or vacation travel.

"Quality time," however, requires more input from you. You have to be seen to be making an effort. Museums are a lot better than they used to be, full of interactive this and that, rather than musty old display cases; art galleries too are brighter, and full of potentially comical modern art that might have been especially made to prick children's curiosity. Board and card games have rather taken a back seat to the computer and the Playstation, but they're not impossible to initiate. Walking is not a universally popular pastime (promises of a stop for an ice cream or milkshake may help); watching movies is a good standby, and one that will allow you a time-out.

However, it may well be that the most valuable way of spending time with your children is in making things, whether it's a tree house, a puppet theatre, a fishing-rod, a dog kennel, a fantasy island, a story, a picture, a song, or a list. As well as being shared activities, these are also emphatically active, and produce results. Together you get to add something new to the world.

209

PAPA SHOWS HIS SON HOW TO BUILD A KITE,
BY B. MIDDERIGH-BOKHORST

# Fun Project: 5

## MAKE A KITE

**1** Mark the shorter rod halfway along, and the longer one a third of the way along. Position the rods at right angles, one on top of the other so that the marks touch. The rods should now form a cross.

**2** With the string, bind the rods together where they meet, tie in a secure knot, and cut off the surplus string.

**3** With a utility knife, cut a small notch into the ends of the rods.

**4** Place some string in the notch at the top of the kite frame and secure it well by winding it around the top of the rod. Then pull the string tightly around the edge of the frame making sure it fits snugly in each notch.

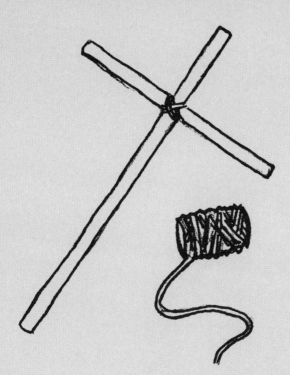

**5** When you get to the top of the frame again, secure the string by tying the ends together in a tight knot.

**6** Lay the finished frame on top of the paper.

**7** Cut the paper around the frame, leaving an excess of approximately 1in/2.5cm around the string.

**8** Apply glue all around the edges of the paper and fold it over so that it encloses the string and sticks to itself within the frame.

**9** Attach a tail to your kite and decorate it with ribbons.

**10** Cut a length of string slightly longer than the length of the shorter rod. Tie the string to each end of the rod.

**11** Repeat step 10 for the longer rod.

**12** At the intersection of these two lengths of string, attach an extra long bridle and get ready to fly your kite!

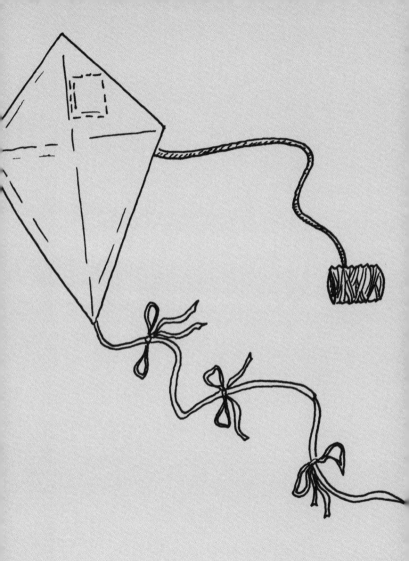

# Woodworking

At one time it used to be said that a knowledge of woodworking was indispensable to a boy. For today's generation of boys and girls, who spend much of their leisure time sitting in front of computer screens or games consoles, the idea of making something consists almost entirely of making a high score.

This may be a controversial statement, but it ought to be a condition of fatherhood that a father should know how to make something out of wood, and to be able to pass on that knowledge to his son or daughter.

You can have fun demonstrating how to use different tools: the best tool kit should include a saw, a plane, a chisel, a gouge, a drawknife, a spokeshave, a ratchet brace, gimlets, bradawls, screwdrivers, a hammer, a mallet, and a gauge. Even as a collection of words they are inspiring. Start by planing, sanding, and polishing an interesting piece of wood to make an ornament. Or craft some wooden jewelry, such as a pendant. As skills are acquired, have a go at slightly more complex constructions. It is best to concentrate on items such as useful boxes, bird houses, dog kennels, rabbit hutches, model ships, and simple pieces of furniture—all things that can be shown off.

The joy of these shared activities cannot be overestimated; working together toward a common goal is a truly bonding experience. You might just get the message across that there are more creative ways to spend time, other than in thrall to a flickering screen.

# Second Youth

Playing ball games with your children, at least before they become too swift, agile, and powerful for you to defeat (in other words while conceding defeat seems like an act of love and encouragement) is great fun. When else in your life have you known that you could win if you so wanted? More fun still, however, is role play. Perhaps for decades you have denied yourself the delicious pleasure of hiding behind a wall, straight as a post, your toy revolver held barrel-up, waiting for the moment to tighten your lips and hurl yourself across the doorway, then roll into the room, yelling "Piaow! Piaow! Piaow!" and thereby wiping out the bad guys and saving the world from imminent destruction. Now of course you are the bad guys, and your six-year-old son, at whom you are shooting, is bawling back, "You're dead, Daddy!" and shooting at you, from behind his bed, with his Ultramegablaster (designed specifically to destroy mechanoid alien dinosaurs).

Swordfighting is considerably more dangerous, though perhaps more romantic. During swordfights it is a good idea to sing, hum, or "da-da" the music of Erich Korngold's score for *The Adventures of Robin Hood* (there is no better swordplay than in this peerless Errol Flynn movie). This gives rhythm and shape to the fight, turning it (almost) into dance—although don't, under any circumstances, mention this to your son. You are less likely to get severely injured by a rap on the knuckles if you are participating in a kind of dance. For your child, who knows full well that there is no possibility of your hurting him, will be quite fearless, not to say ruthless, in the ferocity of his attack. And of course he is, after all, Robin Hood, and therefore the Good Guy. For the father, tactical retreat in a swordfight is never merely an option (in this respect it is quite different from ball games); it is always a necessity. If it looks like your child is resorting to proving his victory by chanting "I won, I won" instead of winning by his superior swordsmanship, the best thing to do is simply to pick him up and turn him upside down until he surrenders.

It is of course tremendously politically incorrect to play weapons games with your children, but this only adds a frisson of wicked delight to the proceedings. Arnold Schwarzenegger would never worry about the neighbors.

"Fatherhood is simply a great excuse to act like a big kid."

# Ball Skills

When advising your children on the proper way to address any kind of ball, remember (a) not to get frustrated when they don't do as you say, and (b) not to get angry at their own impatience with themselves. On the whole, it is probably good to do more watching than talking, during which it is vital to resist all temptation to make faces expressing a smug "told-you-so."

The truth is, teaching your son how to kick or hit a ball can often be deeply unrewarding. It may be that he finds the skill comes quite easily, in which case you may find it hard to congratulate him with quite the required fervor. On the other hand, he might find that it is very hard, and then he will become angry—either with you for not having taught him correctly, or with himself. When you patronizingly praise a less-than-atrocious effort, he will scowl at you, telling you that actually it was garbage. Even then, don't agree.

It's best to leave the business of teaching ball skills to the teachers, and to opt for a little friendly competition with your child instead. It is of course foolish to win these competitions; however, if you are a father who believes that his child should learn disappointment as an important character-building exercise, then at least try to win unemphatically. However, if for example your child turns out to be better than you at table tennis by the age of, say, eleven, use every resource and wile available to you—by dint of experience and the motivating fury of patriarchal jealousy—to win.

"Blessed indeed is the man who hears many
gentle voices calling him father."

LYDIA MARIA CHILD

# Shewing how the art of lying may be taught

WILLIAM WORDSWORTH

I have a boy of five years old,
His face is fair and fresh to see;
His limbs are cast in beauty's mould,
And dearly he loves me.

One morn we stroll'd on our dry walk,
Our quiet house all full in view,
And held such intermitted talk
As we are wont to do.

My thoughts on former pleasures ran;
I thought of Kilve's delightful shore,
My pleasant home, when spring began,
A long, long year before.

A day it was when I could bear
To think, and think, and think again;
With so much happiness to spare,
    I could not feel a pain.

My boy was by my side, so slim
And graceful in his rustic dress!
And oftentimes I talked to him,
    In very idleness.

The young lambs ran a pretty race;
The morning sun shone bright and warm;
"Kilve," said I, "was a pleasant place,
    "And so is Liswyn farm.

"My little boy, which like you more,"
I said and took him by the arm –
"Our home by Kilve's delightful shore,
    "Or here at Liswyn farm?"

"And tell me, had you rather be,"
I said, and held him by the arm,
"At Kilve's smooth shore by the green sea,
    "Or here at Liswyn Farm?"

In careless mood he looked at me,
While still I held him by the arm,
And said, "At Kilve I'd rather be
    "Than here at Liswyn farm."

"Now, little Edward, say why so;
My little Edward, tell me why:"
"I cannot tell, I do not know."
    "Why this is strange," said I.

For here are woods and green-hills warm;
"There surely must some reason be
"Why you would change sweet Liswyn farm
    For Kilve by the green sea."

At this, my boy, so fair and slim,
Hung down his head, nor made reply;
And five times did I say to him,
"Why, Edward, tell me why?"

His head he raised – there was in sight,
It caught his eye, he saw it plain –
Upon the house-top, glittering bright,
A broad and gilded vane.

Then did the boy his tongue unlock,
And thus to me he made reply;
"At Kilve there was no weather-cock,
"And that's the reason why."

Oh dearest, dearest boy! my heart
For better lore would seldom yearn,
Could I but teach the hundredth part
Of what from thee I learn.

# A Walk in the Park

Going for a walk with your children is one of those rare forms of entertainment that costs you nothing. Stealthily, it does you all good. Walks are excellent provokers of talk. The rhythm of movement seems to aid thought, and the constantly changing environment provides excellent subject matter. For those whose habitual view of the world comes from behind a car windshield, it's a great opportunity to take a little exercise.

Walks in the city are always shorter than walks in the country, because there is more occasion to stop. They are also harder on the feet. Then again, they are more easily punctuated by refreshment. A good city walk requires a park, preferably with a statue or two, a shopping street with local stores (with luck featuring a bric-a-brac emporium with unusual wares presented on the sidewalk). A guidebook is useful, but not essential. Shared ignorance and curiosity is a powerful bonding agent, and investigation can be continued at home. A café with an outdoor seating area is also a bonus, where you can sit and guess at the character of passers-by. Hot chocolate, which is both invigorating and comforting, is always popular with children.

The country walk can be anything from a serious hike up a

small mountain, to a civilized stroll along a riverside, or a leisurely wander through woodland. A small book about insects, birds, pebbles, or trees can be handy on these outings, plus a notebook and pen for recording sightings. Incipient explorers may enjoy using a pair of binoculars or even a small telescope; a pocket knife for whittling sticks is also desirable.

If the walk is to take in a mealtime, it can be fun to pack a sack lunch. This is a good excuse to experiment with various sandwich fillings and thrill your children with such concoctions as peanut butter and banana, or cheese and ketchup. Any attempts to bring healthy options to the meal will inevitably be regarded with precocious contempt. It is best to eat all this in the middle of the walk, thereby marking its summit. In ideal circumstances it will be eaten somewhere with a substantial view, and in contemplative silence.

Inclement weather conditions should not really discourage an expedition, although of course tempests featuring lightning or skin-shredding hail are best avoided. Dress to keep out drizzle, and the companionable suffering of such excursions will be amply rewarded in recalled experience.

"My father considered a walk among the mountains as the equivalent of churchgoing."

ALDOUS HUXLEY

# Fun Project: 6

## MAKE A FISHING GAME

**MATERIALS**

Plastic milk containers, or
  other white plastic
  containers
Acrylic paints
Paintbrushes
Waterproof color markers
5 corks
Craft knife (be careful!)
Fine wire scraps
Sticky putty
Garden cane (no sharp
  points)
String, about 1yd/1m
Bowl, filled with water
Scissors

**1** Draw a crab, starfish, octopus, and 2 fish on the white plastic. Cut them out with scissors.

**2** Decorate the sea creatures on both sides with acrylic paint or waterproof color markers. Make them as bright and colorful as you can.

**3** Cut a slit along the length of each cork with a craft knife. (An adult should help you with this.) Slide a creature onto each cork.

**4** Make a loop from a scrap of wire. Twist the ends together. Push the sharp ends into the top of a cork. Repeat for all the creatures.

**5** Press one or 2 small lumps of putty onto the bottom of each creature to make sure it hangs vertically in the water.

**6** Make a hook from a scrap of wire, tie it to the string and tie the end of the string to the cane. Float the creatures in water.

# Father and Son

*by*

EDMUND GOSSE

After one or two brilliant excursions to the sea, winter, in its dampest, muddiest, most languid form, had fallen upon us and shut us in. It was a dreary winter for the wifeless man and the motherless boy. We had come into the house, in precipitate abandonment to that supposed answer to prayer, a great deal too soon. In order to rake together the lump sum for buying it, my Father had denuded himself of almost everything, and our sticks of chairs and tables filled but two or three rooms. Half the little house, or 'villa' as we called it, was not papered, two-thirds were not furnished. The workmen were still finishing the outside when we arrived, and in that connection I recall a little incident which exhibits my Father's morbid delicacy of conscience. He was accustomed in his brighter moments – and this was before the publication of his 'Omphalos' – occasionally to sing loud Dorsetshire songs of his early days, in a strange, broad Wessex lingo that I loved. One October afternoon he and I were sitting on the verandah, and my Father was singing; just around the corner, out of sight, two carpenters were putting up the framework of a greenhouse. In a pause, one of them said to his fellow: "He can zing a zong, zo well's another, though ☞

he be a minister." My Father, who was holding my hand loosely, clutched it, and looking up, I saw his eyes darken. He never sang a secular song again during the whole of his life.

Later in the year, and after his literary misfortune, his conscience became more troublesome than ever. I think he considered the failure of his attempt at the reconciliation of science with religion to have been intended by God as a punishment for something he had done or left undone. In those brooding tramps around and around the garden, his soul was on its knees searching the corners of his conscience for some sin of omission or commission, and one by one every pleasure, every recreation, every trifle scraped out of the dust of past experience, was magnified into a huge offence. He thought that the smallest evidence of levity, the least unbending to human instinct, might be seized by those around him as evidence of inconsistency, and might lead the weaker brethren into offence. The incident of the carpenters and the comic song is typical of a condition of mind which now possessed my Father, in which act after act became taboo, not because each was sinful in itself, but because it might lead others into sin.

I have the conviction that Miss Marks was now mightily afraid of my Father. Whenever she could, she withdrew to the room she called her 'boudoir', a small, chilly apartment, sparsely furnished, looking over what was in process of becoming the vegetable garden. Very properly, that she might have some sanctuary, Miss Marks forbade me to enter this virginal bower, which, of course, became to me an object of harrowing curiosity. Through the key-hole I could see practically nothing; one day I contrived to slip inside, and discovered that there was nothing to see but a plain bedstead and a toilet-table, void of all attraction. In this 'boudoir', on winter afternoons, a fire would be lighted, and Miss Marks would withdraw to it, not seen by us anymore between high-tea and the apocalyptic exercise known as 'worship' – in less strenuous households much less austerely practised under the name of 'family prayers'. Left meanwhile to our own devices, my Father would mainly be reading his book or paper held close up to the candle, while his lips and heavy eyebrows occasionally quivered and palpitated, with literary ardour, in a manner strangely exciting to me. Miss Marks, in a very high cap, and her large teeth shining, would occasionally appear in the doorway, desiring, with spurious geniality, to know how we were 'getting on'. But on these occasions neither of us replied to Miss Marks.

Sometimes in the course of this winter, my Father and I had long cosy talks together over the fire. Our favourite subject was murders. I wonder whether little boys of eight, soon to go upstairs alone at night, often discuss violent crime with a widower-papa? The practice, I cannot help thinking, is unusual; it was, however, consecutive with us. We tried other secular subjects, but we were sure to come around at last to 'what do you suppose they really did with the body?' I was told, a thrilled listener, the adventure of Mrs Manning, who killed a gentleman on the stairs and buried him in quick-lime in the back-kitchen, and it was at this time that I learned the useful historical fact, which abides with me after half a century, that Mrs. Manning was hanged in black satin, which thereupon went wholly out of fashion in England. I also heard about Burke and Hare, whose story nearly froze me into stone with horror.

These were crimes which appear in the chronicles. But who will tell me what 'the Carpet-bag Mystery' was, which my Father and I discussed evening after evening? I have never come across a whisper of it since, and I suspect it of having been a hoax. As I recall the details, people in a boat, passing down the Thames, saw a carpet-bag hung high in air, on one of the projections of a pier of Waterloo Bridge. Being with difficulty dragged down – or perhaps up – this bag was found to be full of human remains, dreadful butcher's business of joints and fragments. Persons were missed, were identified, were again denied – the whole is a vapour in my memory which shifts as I try to define it. But clear enough is the picture I hold of myself, in a high chair, on the left-hand side of the sitting-room fireplace, the leaping flames reflected in the glass-case of tropical insects on the opposite wall, and my Father, leaning anxiously forward, with uplifted finger, emphasizing to me the pros and cons of the horrible carpet-bag evidence. I suppose that my interest in these discussions – and Heaven knows I was animated enough – amused and distracted my Father, whose idea of a suitable theme for childhood's ear now seems to me surprising. I soon found that these subjects were not welcome to everybody, for, starting the Carpet-bag Mystery one morning with Miss Marks, in the hope of delaying my arithmetic lesson, she fairly threw her apron over her ears, and told me, from that vantage, that if I did not desist at once, she should scream.

Occasionally we took winter walks together, my Father and I, down some lane that led to a sight of the sea, or over the rolling downs. We tried to recapture the charm of those delightful strolls in London, when we used to lean over the bridges and watch the ducks. But we could not recover this pleasure. My Father was deeply enwoven in the chain of his own thoughts, and would stalk on, without a word, buried in angry reverie. If he spoke to me, on these excursions, it was a pain to me to answer him. I could talk on easy terms with him indoors, seated in my high chair, with our heads on a level, but it was intolerably laborious to look up into the firmament and converse with a dark face against the sky. The actual exercise of walking, too, was very exhausting to me; the bright red mud, to the strange colour of which I could not for a long while get accustomed, becoming caked about my little shoes, and wearying me extremely. I would grow petulant and cross, contradict my Father, and oppose his whims. These walks were distressing to us both, yet he did not like to walk alone, and he had no other friend. However, as the winter advanced, they had to be abandoned, and the habit of our taking a 'constitutional' together was never resumed.

"I associate the smell of new-cut grass with my father, and sunny days, and happiness."

NATASHA BURNS

# Fun Project: 7

## MAKE A CORK RAFT

> **MATERIALS**
> 4 corks
> Colored paper,
> small sheets
> Stickers
> 2 plastic drinking
> straws
> Utility knife (be
> careful!)
> Scissors
> Waterproof
> glue

**1** Glue the corks side by side to form the raft. Press them together firmly until the glue is completely dry.

**2** Cut 2 square sails from paper about the length of a cork, and decorate them with stickers. Cut 2 flags from paper and add stickers for decoration.

**3** With the utility knife, cut a slit at the top and bottom of each sail, in the center. (An adult should help you with this.) Thread a straw through each slit. Glue a flag to the top of each straw mast.

**4** Cut a small slit in the middle of 2 corks. Cut the straws to the right length. Flatten the cut ends and push each into a slit. Glue the straw masts in place.

# Happy Campers!

There is a kind of Woodstock-fueled myth that camping is a way of getting in touch with your inner self, of communing with nature and releasing the eternal spirit. That approach may be fine for a long weekend of youthful self-indulgence, but it certainly isn't practical for a summer vacation with the family.

Camping can be a wonderful experience for your offspring, and that is likely to make it a wonderful experience for you. The quality of the camping experience relies on thorough preparation. If you're not organized, your children will forever think of camping as grimy, squalid, hard work, and boring. But if you prepare well, the family will have the vacation of a lifetime; on top of that, there is the profound added value of being able to share chores together.

The big problem with camping is rain. Rain is evil. Rain makes things damp, and this means you're wet even after the rain has gone. So you need to put up the tent correctly—absolutely correctly.

Putting up a tent is not straightforward. It is never straightforward, despite what your goes-camping-four-times-a-year friend tells you. What is more, although you will remember to take the instruction manual on the first outing, you will leave it behind on the second and find that you have to work from memory. This is disastrous because (a) mother, father, son, and daughter will all have quite different memories, and (b) all their memories will be wrong. Nevertheless, after four, five, six, seven, or fifteen attempts, the modern tent does settle into its intended form, and it will keep out the rain.

Don't forget to take proper shoes. Espadrilles are all very well when shuffling about in sunshine upon a bed of dry pine needles, but rain can churn up the ground very quickly.

The great joy of camping is, it has to be said, children. On a large campsite there will be herds of children forever wandering around the place, apparently attached to no particular parents, getting in the way of people trying to walk in a straight line (known as adults), and loving their freedom. If you have done your homework properly, the campsite will have an impressive adult-unfriendly swimming pool with chutes, slides, bridges, and channels. There will also be playgrounds, climbing frames, table tennis facilities, tennis courts, and a pool; also bicycles for hire and sundry other ways of distracting children from the enjoyable pursuit of badgering their parents.

If you're camping in the wild then you are probably going to have to provide most of this entertainment yourself. With one child this is of course fantastic fun but it is almost impossible with any number higher than one. Take a Swiss Army Knife with everything on it (magnifying glass, tweezers, encyclopedia of flora and fauna) and teach your child how to use it.

The distractions of the day are probably going to be as nothing compared with the deep pleasures of the night. Teach your children how to light a campfire, and how to play the guitar; lie brazenly about your knowledge of the stars. Cook fish you have caught during the day, or (more likely) warm up a can of beans. Whatever you eat will be delicious, and you will have taught your children that it isn't absolutely necessary to live in a house.

"Camping is a great opportunity for Dad to use his caveman instincts to provide food and shelter for his family."

# Dad's Favorite Recipe: 4

## SCRAMBLED EGGS

Caroline French Benton's recipe for scrambled eggs (from *The Fun of Cooking*) is so charming it will have the kids contemplating the exact size of a hickory nut...

> **INGREDIENTS**
> 1 egg for each person
> 2 tablespoons of milk to each egg
> 2 shakes of salt
> 1 shake of pepper

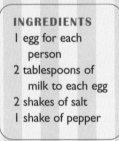

"Break the eggs in a bowl, beat them twelve times, then add the milk, salt and pepper; heat a pan, put in a piece of butter the size of a hickory nut, and when it is melted, pour in the eggs; stir them as they cook, and scrape them off the bottom of the pan; when they are all thick and creamy, they are done."

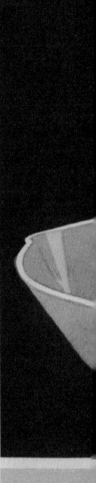

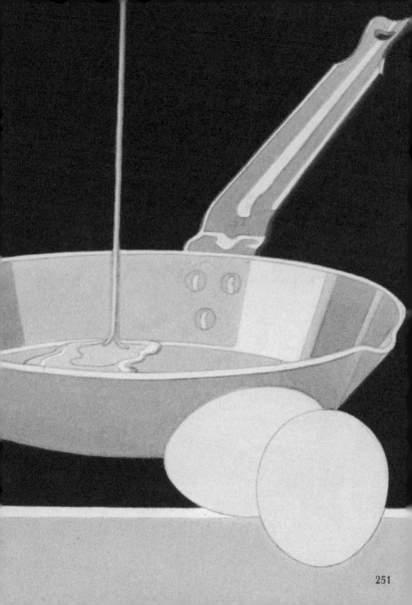

# Rainy Days

You are walking in the mountains with your father. The day that began blue, bright, and breezy has turned slate-gray, and rain is falling. "A shower," he asserts confidently. "It will pass." You believe this because you want to, although the sky is descending in every direction like a foul night.

Soon you are drenched to the skin. Your father declares that the weather is terrific. Which it is, lowering and inhospitable; but he means he is enjoying it. And soon you too are enjoying it, for you are as wet as it is possible to be. You can be no wetter. There is nothing further this rain can do to you. Your clothes are plastered to your body, but your pace is keeping you warm, and your father's inevitable singing (nonsensical words to the tune of the William Tell Overture) keeps your spirits high.

You have never been exposed to the elements like this before. And that is the point. Your father knows this; knows how valuable the experience can be if properly handled. By the time you clatter home, squelching all over the kitchen floor, it has become the most memorable walk of your life. Your mother rushes you upstairs, where you get under a hot shower with manly glee. The meal that follows is a meal of the gods. And this is what your father can give you that a mere companion cannot: the desire to turn misfortune to the good.

# Celebrity Fathers

George W. Bush may well be the most famous living offspring of a famous father, but the world of celebrity expands with each new launch of a magazine devoted to its camera-loving denizens. Some of them are even talented. The Fonda dynasty of actors has given us Henry (father), Jane, Peter, and Bridget. The actor Jon Voight has given us the undeniable charms of his daughter Angelina Jolie, well known for her role as the computer-generated icon beloved by teenage boys, Lara Croft.

Elvis Presley's daughter, Lisa Marie, is not exactly a pop princess, but she has a respectable voice. Mick Jagger's eldest daughter, Jade, is frequently seen at fashionable events along with a coterie of famous friends including John Lennon's son, Julian; meanwhile, Sir Paul McCartney's daughter, Stella, is a queen of fashion. That great showman Steve Tyler, lead singer of the ageless rock band Aerosmith, has produced perhaps his most beautiful work in the form of the peerless model and actress Liv Tyler.

Another well-known dynasty of actors originated in the nineteenth century. Maurice Barrymore, an Englishman born in India, married Georgiana Drew of Philadelphia. They had three astonishing children, John, Lionel, and Ethel, who all became award-winning actors. John's son also became an actor: under the name John Drew, he starred in *When the City Sleeps*. In 1975 he had a daughter. She starred in her first movie, *E.T.* at the age of six. Her name is Drew Barrymore.

But perhaps most remarkable of all celebrity children of celebrity fathers is Laila Ali, a women's boxing champion, and daughter of The Greatest himself, Muhammad Ali.

# The Children of Zeus

Zeus, the supreme god of Greek mythology, had at least thirty-six children. They were not, however, all born to his wife Hera (with whom he had Ares, Hebe, Hephaestus, and Eileithyia).

With Mnemosyne he had nine children known collectively as the Muses. Each promoted an area of the arts. They were: Clio (history), Euterpe (flute playing), Thalia (comedy), Melpomene (tragedy), Terpsichore (dance), Erato (love poetry), Polyhymnia (sacred music), Urania (astrology), and Calliope (epic poetry).

By Euronyme Zeus fathered the Graces—Aglaia (splendor), Euphrosyne (mirth), and Thalia (rejoicing); and by Themis the Fates—Clotho, Lachesis, and Atropos. The Fates had special responsibilities: the thread of life was said to be woven by Clotho, measured by Lachesis, and, finally, severed by Atropos.

Zeus also fathered most of the gods and goddesses that are very familiar to us: Heracles, Perseus, Persephone, Aphrodite, Hermes, Athene, Dionysus, Apollo, and Artemis (born to Leto), and that same Helen that caused all the difficulties for Menelaus, Agamemnon, Odysseus, and Achilles, not to mention poor Priam and Hector.

It is fairly unlikely that Zeus was a particularly attentive father. He was clearly often busy with the making of new children and of course he had to spend a great deal of his time dealing with wrongdoers, dispensing justice, and hurling thunderbolts. We shouldn't be too hard on him, however, because he had a challenging childhood—he had to kill his own father, Cronus, in order to survive (Cronus had eaten all Zeus's brothers and sisters).

# Vacation Time

For a vacation, children love to go to the same place over and over again and do the same things. They enjoy having an inbuilt knowledge of a second world. This should be very much encouraged, because it allows you time to (a) sleep, (b) relax, and (c) sleep. Take a book—you won't read it, but it will help you achieve (a) and (c) so long as it is not too exciting. Thomas Mann is useful in these situations. He was a very earnest German novelist of very long books.

The mother is likely to want to go to new places, to see different things, and explore strange new worlds. There is a solution to this, which is to agree to one such vacation a year. All parties will be satisfied, except that the children will invariably want to return to Venice/Vermont/Vietnam the following weekend.

It may not be a universal phenomenon, but it is quite often the case that the father will take on the responsibility for weatherproofing his family. He will apply the sunblock, make sure the waterproofs are stowed, towel down his children when they come out of the ocean shivering, and so on. The organizational imperative is at work here, a military attitude to the business of going places that requires one to be prepared for any eventuality. A man will almost always prefer to rely on his own resources than upon the comfort of strangers. That is both his strength and his weakness.

"All the feeling which my father could not put into words was in his hand—any dog, child, or horse would recognize the kindness of it."

FREYA STARK

# Help! Missing on the Beach

Your younger son goes missing on the beach. Ten frantic minutes ensue, the panic growing heavy in the pit of your stomach. You hide this from the boy's mother as though it were the secret codeword to unleash the world's entire nuclear arsenal, and she were Dr. Strangelove. Fathers must remain cool in a crisis.

Eventually, your son wanders nonchalantly into view. He has been counting sand. What number did he get up to? Twenty-nine. You are delighted and issue a mild warning not to do that sort of thing again.

His elder brother approaches. He looks cross.

"Why didn't you tell him off?"

"I did tell him off."

"No you didn't. You weren't cross. You didn't tell him off like you'd tell me off. You didn't tell him off like you told me off when I went for a walk in the park."

"That was different."

"No it wasn't."

You hesitate, and then realize that actually he's right. Your panic about his missing brother, awful though it was, had been slight compared to the anguish that would have gripped you if the elder boy had gone missing. And so you decide to do something you don't do often enough: you open yourself up a little to your son.

You explain that he and his brother have different characters and are likely to disappear for different reasons. You risk being honest: "If you had disappeared, I'd know it was probably because you were lost. If your brother had disappeared, I'd think he was probably exploring." Silence. "He's more resourceful than you; he hasn't been cosseted."

"What's cosseted?"

"You've been over-protected." Silence. He may not like the meaning of your words, but he likes being talked to in this way. You tell him that he, as the elder son, will always be expected to be more responsible, or rather that expectations will always seem greater. It is simply a function of age. What is more, his brother will always expect his protection. He nods. He knows that it is one of the responsibilities of love.

# Swimming Lessons

One of the most effective methods of ensuring that your child has a lifetime's fear of water is to enter a bleak ocean from a shingle beach, backwards, the breakers cracking over your back as you do so. The child, believing all his father does is right and good, will tend to imitate the action of this tigerish parent and soon find himself dashed into the unforgiving pebbles of the beach, with a mouth full of icy brine and swimming trunks full of coarse sand.

If, however, the sea is calm and the sun bright, the father may use a different method, whereby he approaches the child as though from the bottomless deep, with no apparent means of locomotion, making curious gurgling noises, and with an expression of weird ferocity around his eyebrows. This will either terrify the child or cause him to have a fit of giggling. In either case it he is likely to take in a whole lot of seawater and exit the ocean spluttering, desperately in search of a towel and, more importantly, his mom.

# Building a Sandcastle

There are certain things that every father should know about sandcastles. The perfect sandcastle must be built while the tide is rising, otherwise it will not be destroyed. (The first rule of sandcastle-building is that the sandcastle must be destroyed.) A sandcastle is like food: it is made to be consumed.

Proper tools—the time-honored bucket and spade—are essential. Moreover, the tools should be sturdy because there is nothing worse than getting to the beach with a handful of excited children, finding the perfect spot to begin work on the sandcastle, sticking the spade into the sand for the first scoop, and then finding it snap in two to the sounds of wailing children. Buckets should not be too large, because children must be able to fill them and turn them over. The sand should be fine, but not too dry. For an impressive castle, which will blow other dads' efforts out of the water, an area about six feet square is required, although it is probably easier to demark a circular area, by dragging the spade around you. Gather some pebbles and shells for decoration; seaweed, too, can be usefully employed in this respect.

Do not smile or laugh during the preparatory period. It cannot be stressed too strongly that building a sandcastle is a very serious business. You don't laugh when you play chess, do you? No.

There is a proper order to the construction process. First of all, build a moat and a hill. The sand excavated from the moat goes into the center of the circle. The hill is then flattened and the castle is built on top. Relatively straightforward, you would have thought. Not at all. The second rule of sandcastle-building is that a sandcastle is never finished. A wall can be erected on the outside of the moat, punctuated by new towers. Or crenulations may be added to the inner walls. The aforementioned shells, pebbles, and seaweed may be employed to suggest regal affluence and Medici-like aspirations. Meanwhile, long ditches can be dug down to the incoming sea, to encourage water into the moat. These too can then be given further protection, additional towers, and additional turrets.

Eventually, the sea sweeps in toward the castle and now the work becomes truly hard and frantic. With a hope that is of course utterly forlorn, but with great enjoyment, children and parents desperately attempt to keep the ocean at bay. New ramparts are laid as the briny sea destroys fortifications. There is screaming, frantic instructions, and, at last, laughter. The tide will not be held, and soon the living architecture is smoothed into a ghostly mound, which eventually melts away to nothing, extinguished from existence like the legendary island of Atlantis. Now you can swim, and feel the salt of the sea cut away the sweat and sand from your back, shins, and forearms.

The family has been submerged in—and united through—the work, the process, the traveling; not the arriving. This is the lesson of the sandcastle. Life may be a journey across shifting sands, but it is possible to construct a path with firm foundations.

"Dad's great about showing us how to do stuff. Even if he doesn't really know what he's doing, he passes that knowledge on to us."

DAVID BUTLER

# The Secret Garden

*by*

FRANCES HODGSON BURNETT

The ivy hung thick over the door, the key was buried under the shrubs, no human being had passed that portal for ten lonely years—and yet inside the garden there were sounds. They were the sounds of running scuffling feet seeming to chase round and round under the trees, they were strange sounds of lowered suppressed voices—exclamations and smothered joyous cries. It seemed actually like the laughter of young things, the uncontrollable laughter of children who were trying not to be heard but who in a moment or so—as their excitement mounted—would burst forth. What in heaven's name was he dreaming of—what in heaven's name did he hear? Was he losing his reason and thinking he heard things which were not for human ears? What was it that the far clear voice had meant?

And then the moment came, the uncontrollable moment when the sounds forgot to hush themselves. The feet ran faster and faster—they were nearing the garden door—there was quick strong young breathing and a wild outbreak of laughing shows which could not be contained—and the door in the wall was flung wide open, the sheet of ivy swinging back, and a boy burst through it at full speed and, without seeing the ☞

outsider, dashed almost into his arms.

Mr. Craven had extended them just in time to save him from falling as a result of his unseeing dash against him, and when he held him away to look at him in amazement at his being there he truly gasped for breath.

He was a tall boy and a handsome one. He was glowing with life and his running had sent splendid color leaping to his face. He threw the thick hair back from his forehead and lifted a pair of strange gray eyes—eyes full of boyish laughter and rimmed with black lashes like a fringe. It was the eyes which made Mr. Craven gasp for breath. "Who—What? Who!" he stammered.

This was not what Colin had expected—this was not what he had planned. He had never thought of such a meeting. And yet to come dashing out—winning a race—perhaps it was even better. He drew himself up to his very tallest. Mary, who had been running with him and had dashed through the door too, believed that he managed to make himself look taller than he had ever looked before—inches taller.

"Father," he said, "I'm Colin. You can't believe it. I scarcely can myself. I'm Colin."

Like Mrs. Medlock, he did not understand what his father meant when he said hurriedly:

"In the garden! In the garden!"

"Yes," hurried on Colin. "It was the garden that did it—and Mary and Dickon and the creatures—and the Magic.

No one knows. We kept it to tell you when you came. I'm well, I can beat Mary in a race. I'm going to be an athlete."

He said it all so like a healthy boy—his face flushed, his words tumbling over each other in his eagerness—that Mr. Craven's soul shook with unbelieving joy.

Colin put out his hand and laid it on his father's arm.

"Aren't you glad, Father?" he ended. "Aren't you glad? I'm going to live forever and ever and ever!"

Mr. Craven put his hands on both the boy's shoulders and held him still. He knew he dared not even try to speak for a moment.

"Take me into the garden, my boy," he said at last. "And tell me all about it."

And so they led him in.

The place was a wilderness of autumn gold and purple and violet blue and flaming scarlet and on every side were sheaves of late lilies standing together—lilies which were white or white and ruby. He remembered well when the first of them had been planted that just at this season of the year their late glories should reveal themselves. Late roses climbed and hung and clustered and the sunshine deepening the hue of the yellowing trees made one feel that one stood in an embowered temple of gold. The newcomer stood silent just as the children had done when they came into its grayness. He looked round and round.

"I thought it would be dead," he said.

"Mary thought so at first," said Colin. "But it came alive."

Then they sat down under their tree—all but Colin, who wanted to stand while he told the story.

It was the strangest thing he had ever heard, Archibald ☞

Craven thought, as it was poured forth in headlong boy fashion. Mystery and Magic and wild creatures, the weird midnight meeting—the coming of the spring—the passion of insulted pride which had dragged the young Rajah to his feet to defy old Ben Weatherstaff to his face. The odd companionship, the play acting, the great secret so carefully kept. The listener laughed until tears came into his eyes and sometimes tears came into his eyes when he was not laughing. The Athlete, the Lecturer, the Scientific Discoverer was a laughable, lovable, healthy young human thing.

"Now," he said at the end of the story, "it need not be a secret any more. I dare say it will frighten them nearly into fits when they see me—but I am never going to get into the chair again. I shall walk back with you, Father—to the house."

Ben Weatherstaff's duties rarely took him away from the gardens, but on this occasion he made an excuse to carry some vegetables to the kitchen and being invited into the servants' hall by Mrs. Medlock to drink a glass of beer he was on the spot—as he had hoped to be—when the most dramatic event Misselthwaite Manor had seen during the present generation actually took place. One of the windows looking upon the courtyard gave also a glimpse of the lawn. Mrs. Medlock, knowing Ben had come from the gardens, hoped that he might have caught sight of his master and even by chance of his meeting with Master Colin.

"Did you see either of them, Weatherstaff?" she asked.

Ben took his beer-mug from his mouth and wiped his lips with the back of his hand.

"Aye, that I did," he answered with a shrewdly significant air.

"Both of them?" suggested Mrs. Medlock.

"Both of 'em," returned Ben Weatherstaff. "Thank ye kindly, ma'am, I could sup up another mug of it."

"Together?" said Mrs. Medlock, hastily overfilling his beer-mug in her excitement.

"Together, ma'am," and Ben gulped down half of his new mug at one gulp.

"Where was Master Colin? How did he look? What did they say to each other?"

"I didna' hear that," said Ben, "along o' only bein' on th' stepladder lookin', over th' wall. But I'll tell thee this. There's been things goin' on outside as you house people knows nowt about. An' what tha'll find out tha'll find out soon."

And it was not two minutes before he swallowed the last of his beer and waved his mug solemnly toward the window which took in through the shrubbery a piece of the lawn.

"Look there," he said, "if tha's curious. Look what's comin' across th' grass."

When Mrs. Medlock looked she threw up her hands and gave a little shriek and every man and woman servant within hearing bolted across the servants' hall and stood looking through the window with their eyes almost starting out of their heads.

Across the lawn came the Master of Misselthwaite and he looked as many of them had never seen him. And by his side, with his head up in the air and his eyes full of laughter walked as strongly and steadily as any boy in Yorkshire—Master Colin.

# Fun Project: 8

## MAKE A MINIATURE GARDEN

### MATERIALS

Wooden fruit crate
Popsicle sticks, cut in half
2 beads, 2 buttons
Paints and paintbrushes
Color markers
Dried split peas or lentils,
    or both
Aluminum foil
Assorted colored paper

Wooden skewer, cut in half
Fabric and yarn
Matchbox drawer
Matchsticks
Cotton reel, cork
Paper clip
Cocktail paper umbrella
Scissors
Glue

**1** Glue popsicle sticks – rounded end up – around the crate to make a fence and gates. Glue bead handles on the gates.

**2** On the base of the crate, draw a path and paint glue on it. Pour split peas onto the path to cover it. Shake off the extra split peas.

**3** Paint the rest of the base green for grass. Glue on a pond cut from foil, and glue on yellow paper fish to swim in it.

**4** Glue a bead to one end of each piece of skewer. Glue the skewers to opposite corners of the crate. Glue tiny fabric clothes to yarn. Tie the yarn to the skewers.

**5** For the wheelbarrow, glue button wheels on a matchbox and add matchstick handles. For the table, glue a fabric tablecloth onto the reel, and push the umbrella through a tiny hole in the middle.

**6** The cat is a painted cork with glued-on matchstick legs, paper ears, and a yarn tail. For the butterfly, fix a paper clip body to wings cut from blue paper.

# Like Father, Like Son

*"A man's desire for a son is usually nothing but the wish to duplicate himself in order that such a remarkable pattern may not be lost to the world."*

HELEN ROWLAND

The son's father was a great man: important, respected, loved. The boy felt shy and small in the world. He was always afraid of failure. The father was also a good man: upright and moral (but not sanctimonious). He never told lies.

The boy felt himself to be low and sly. The father was a popular man. His laugh was recognized far and wide; he was welcomed by friends on three continents. The boy liked to keep himself to himself, had few close friends, and never encouraged acquaintance. The father was also a war hero, his gallantry rewarded with medals; the son thought himself a coward. The son admired and respected the father.

On his deathbed, the father said, "You are just like me," and because the son knew his father would not lie, he believed him, and love was born.

# On My First Son

BEN JONSON

Farewell, thou child of my right hand, and joy;
My sin was too much hope of thee, lov'd boy.
Seven years thou wert lent to me, and I thee pay,
Exacted by thy fate, on the just day.
Oh, could I lose all father now! For why
Will man lament the state he should envy?
To have so soon 'scaped world's and flesh's rage,
And if no other misery, yet age!
Rest in soft peace, and, asked, say, Here doth lie
Ben Jonson his best piece of poetry.
For whose sake henceforth all his vows be such
As what he loves may never like too much.

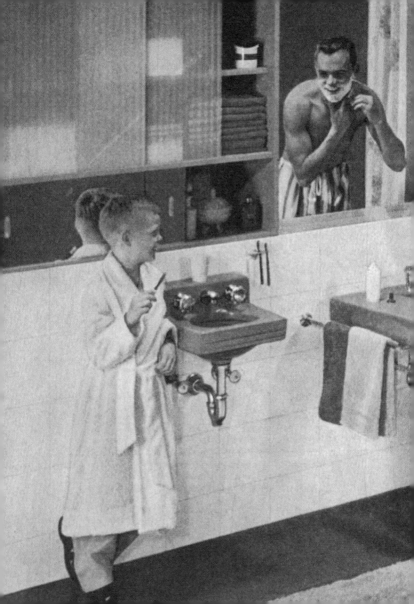

"Traditionally, the defining moment in a man's life arrives when he looks in his shaving glass and finds his father staring back."

DON PATERSON

# Shoeshine Boys

An important function of fatherhood is teaching your son how to polish his shoes. This is a dying tradition, employing a dying craft, due to the remorseless advance of casual shoes and sneakers. Nevertheless, like other manly traditions—such as walking on the road side of the sidewalk when accompanying a lady, and insisting that a lady sits facing into the restaurant—this tradition should be passed down to your son on the grounds that it is easier to break the rules once you know what they are.

Polishing shoes requires, above all, an Old Box. This will have been passed down from generation to generation. It will contain ancient tins of polish, utterly dried-up and useless (but picturesque and redolent of another age), some grubby-looking sponges and cloths unwashed in aeons (fathers don't wash cloths), and a selection of wire brushes. There may even be an ill-used toothbrush hidden at the bottom. There will certainly be an unused tube of suede cream, untouched since around 1972.

The actual polishing procedure has a moral dimension—how much sweat are you willing to put into the task? The fact is that it becomes obsessive, which is why fathers used to enjoy it so much. Just like the ritualistic cleaning of the car, there was no excuse for the work not to be perfect. Entire mornings could be spent removing dirt, applying polish, and, well, polishing.

Your son will resent every moment spent on this task, and in twenty years' time he will impose it on his own offspring.

# Hurtful Words

The middle son had behaved perfectly all day long, helping to do the dishes, cleaning the stove, and making useful suggestions for his father's work. He was a delight to be with. In the afternoon his father took him, along with his older and younger brother, to a local go-kart track. Although he was only ten years old, he was already an accomplished go-kart driver. His driving was fearless and confident, and he was light in the car, with no weight to hold back the vehicle. His father watched as he sped around the track, lapping his brothers, and sailing past other teenagers who would leave the track unhappy at being whupped by a whippersnapper. His father was proud.

Back at home, the three brothers decided to form a band. To supplement their guitar and keyboards, they fashioned drums out of pots, pans, and boxes. An atrocious noise ensued. For two hours, the father enjoyed and endured the sound of his sons molding themselves into a rock band. The middle boy led the way, urging them on, wanting a result, unwilling to settle for chaos. His father realized that go-karting was not the only thing the boy was good at.

At the end of the evening, the father suggested the boys might like to watch a film before bedtime. "Let's watch this," said the elder brother, looking through the DVD selection and pulling out a film.

"No, we have to discuss it," said the middle brother.

"Yes, and then when you have talked about it together for an hour, you will end up watching what you want to watch," said the father, gesturing toward his middle son.

The middle son thought about smiling, and then felt hurt; often he would take these barbs as a kind of compliment. Now he couldn't disguise his pain. He ran upstairs to his bedroom, and nothing would persuade him to come down.

The father tried to apologize. When he went to bed, he thought over the incident. Why had he said it? Maybe because the boy had been so well-behaved, so successful, all day. He had even looked perfect. Maybe something inside the father had thought this was dangerous, that perfection was to be avoided, and that the boy needed to be brought down a peg or two. And as soon as he put it to himself like that, he realized how cruel he had been. Where he should have praised the brothers, he had instead decided to upbraid the middle boy. He resolved to find some way of apologizing, a way that wasn't simply spoken words. Maybe the written word would do the trick…

"Every father should remember that one day his son will follow his example instead of his advice."

ANONYMOUS

# The Noble Soldier

The infantry captain had a soldier in his company that he could not understand. The captain liked to understand his men, because he thought it important to know what qualities you could rely on in the various situations of battle, but he was unable to work out whether the soldier was very brave or very foolhardy in his actions. He was never sure whether to reward or scold him.

One day the soldier was killed, in ignoble circumstances. He had been running away. The captain had to file his despatch. He did not know whether to describe the true circumstances in which the soldier died, or whether to substitute a different occasion that demonstrated the soldier's bravery. The captain was sure of only one thing, and that was that the soldier did not deserve to be remembered as a coward.

He wrote to ask the opinion of his own father, who had also been a soldier, and who was a just, kind, and noble man. His father replied that the distinction between bravery and foolhardiness was impossible to make; that the soldier should be put up for a posthumous award for gallantry; and that the circumstances in which the award had been earned should be entirely fictional (indeed they should be made extreme). The captain's despatch should contain no room for doubt that the soldier deserved an award.

The lesson the father taught the captain was twofold. One was that bravery could be folly; the other was that in the service of truth it is sometimes necessary to lie, and that if you are going to lie in order to achieve the truth, you should tell enormous lies.

# Dad's Favorite Recipe: 5

## CLUB SANDWICHES

This superior sandwich is quick to make and hugely satisfying. It's one meal your kids could make for you, for once!

**INGREDIENTS**
6 slices good quality
　　white bread
butter (optional)
4–6 tbsp good quality
　　mayonnaise
4–6 crisp lettuce leaves
2 ripe tomatoes, sliced
8 rindless bacon slices
　　(rashers),
cooked until crisp
6oz/175g cooked
　　chicken breast,
　　sliced

**TO SERVE**
bread-and-butter pickle
　　or chutney
potato chips (crisps)

**1** Lightly toast the bread. Butter each slice on one side only, if required. Lay 2 slices on a cutting board or work surface.

**2** Spread each slice with mayonnaise and cover with 2 or 3 lettuce leaves; add slices of tomato, and 2 bacon slices. Top each with a second slice of toast, spread with more mayonnaise and add another lettuce leaf. Cover evenly with slices of chicken breast. Cover with the remaining slices of toast, buttered sides down.

**3** Cut each sandwich into 4 triangles and secure each triangle with a toothpick. Arrange on plates and serve immediately, with the pickles and potato chips on the side.

# A Man's Prerogative

Most of the important things that we teach our children are taught by example, and thankfully these usually do not require conscious preparation. Fathers have a special role in their son's education in this respect. Without ever being instructed, the boy will learn how to Leave The Toilet Seat Up; he will learn to Hog The Remote; he will discover The Art Of Not Being Able To Find Things; and it may even be nature rather than nurture that will ensure that he absorbs the rule that Being Lost Is Infinitely Preferable To Asking For Directions.

The Ability To Not Fold Clothes is essential to the male sex, which, on the whole, prefers not to change clothes at all. Another not unrelated subject is mud, probably the most omnipresent of the earth's natural bounties in a growing boy's life. Getting Mud Everywhere does require occasional demonstration. Most fathers will remember how it is done without too much prompting. Hints may also be needed for the indelicate business of Walking So Briskly That Nobody Has Time To Stop And Look At Anything, an ability almost all fathers possess, but which nevertheless has to be done properly—unlike the dishes, which can dry on their own, for goodness sake!

# A Very Tall Boy

## The One Lone Limerick of Uncle Sidney's

JAMES WHITCOMB RILEY

*Some credulous chroniclers tell us*
*Of a very tall youngster named Ellis*
*Whose Pa said, "Ma-ri-er,*
*If Bubb grows much higher,*
*He'll have to be trained up a trellis."*

# Bonding with Dad

Tom hated being woken up on those cold winter mornings. It was still dark after all, still night! But the animals had to be checked, and for some reason his dad always chose him to help, rather than either of two older brothers. He would climb unsteadily into his jeans, so cold they felt damp, pull on a warm top, dig his feet into thick socks and boots, and join his father in the kitchen, where a steaming mug of coffee and breakfast would be waiting. After this sustenance, Tom didn't hate the morning so much.

Their daily task was to check the safety and comfort of the livestock, and although occasionally his dad would show him practical stuff such as how to free a trapped ewe, approach a heifer, tie a knot, or climb a rope ladder, mostly he talked—as they dealt with more mundane chores—about his life, and what he had learned from his experiences. He covered war and peace, poverty and comfort, love and hate. Big things. Tom would watch his father's breath in the morning air, and the little clouds he expelled seemed to describe the world to the child.

When the three boys grew up, the two older brothers became farmers. But Tom became a teacher.

# Bach and Sons

Johann Sebastian Bach (1685–1750) is arguably the greatest composer that has ever lived. He grew up in Eisenach in Germany, where his father was the director of music for the town. Johann married twice and had twenty children, four of whom were highly respected composers in their own right.

J. S. Bach married his first wife, Maria Barbara Bach, a distant cousin, in 1709. Two sons from this marriage became distinguished musicians. Wilhelm Friedemann Bach became known as the "Halle Bach" after he was made the chief organist of that town. Carl Philipp Emmanuel Bach was appointed, in his twenties, as court musician to Crown Prince Frederick of Prussia; and in 1767 he succeeded his godfather Georg Telemann as music director of Hamburg.

Maria Barbara died in 1720, and Bach married Anna Magdalena Wilcke. Two of their sons became celebrated. Johann Christoph Friedrich became court composer in Bückeberg (and father of yet another composer, Wilhelm Friedrich Ernst Bach); and Johann Christian Bach was the "London Bach," appointed to the service of the Queen of England. In 1764, in London, he met and instructed the young Mozart.

All four of these musically gifted Bach children were taught exclusively by their father.

# Back from Work

What was it that Father brought home from the office in his old, worn briefcase? It wasn't just paperwork, a primitive calculator, and an uneaten apple. It was laughter, flattery, the ridiculous, the lifting of the mundane into the vivid present. He brought home his vigor, vim, and valor, to side with his children against their teachers; he also brought home his inability to do long-division math. He brought home his knowledge of the idiosyncrasies of the Roman emperors; his love of music, of Duke Ellington and Handel. He brought home his love of stories—sad and joyful, long and short, true and truer (all stories being true, so long as they were good). He brought home his inability to adjust the TV properly, and his comedy show of parsimony with fine wine. And he brought home the roughness of his skin, the hair on his neck, his man's hard hands. He brought his love and his pleasure at being once more with his family. He brought home the world.

"Sometimes the person I want to see more than anyone in the world is my dad."

SHARON DENNIS WYETH

# Picture Credits

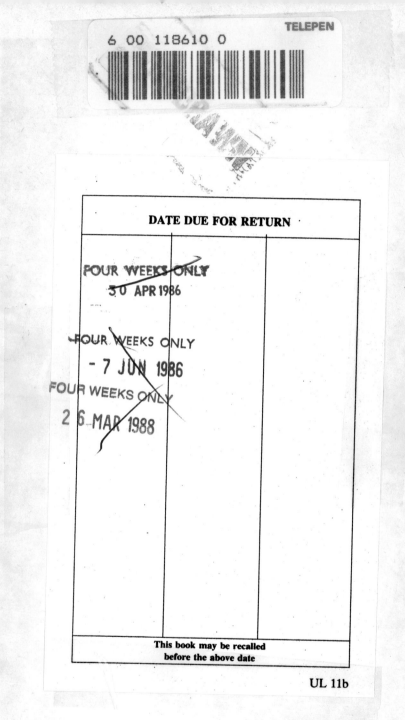